attacked before the German ⟨...⟩ s and troops now stationed at Channel p⟨...⟩

Yet, as terrifying as it was – overall, British c⟨...⟩ nbered 1,556 – like the Blitz before it, Operation Steinbock achieved very little in military terms. Indeed, this time damage to property and industry was minimal and a combination of inexperienced German aircrews and superior British defences saw the Luftwaffe lose 329 aircraft (234 shot down by RAF night fighters; 95 by anti-aircraft fire) before Operation Steinbock was abandoned in May 1944, having failed to hamper the Allies' preparations for the invasion of Occupied Europe.

By the end of 1943, people in Britain had felt that victory could soon be within the Allies' grasp as the tide of war turned in their favour. The end of the North African campaign, and the sweep from the beaches of Salerno and Anzio into Italy, had left the Allies with the opportunity and the resources to stage the operation for which everyone was waiting – the invasion of Occupied France.

By the spring of 1944, it seemed that this could not be far off. National Fire Service personnel, together with barrage balloons and heavy anti-aircraft batteries, were moved southwards to defend ports on the South Coast where huge numbers of Allied troops were concentrated. The defence of many towns and cities was left with the local Home Guard units and their 'Z' rocket batteries.

Road and rail traffic southwards increased, and canvas covers could not disguise the tell-tale shapes of landing craft. Column after column of tanks and armoured cars snaked their way around urban outskirts, all heading south, and military camps all over Britain became deserted as the invasion army was assembled.

That there would be an invasion was no secret. In March 1944, to mark the beginning of 'Salute the Soldier Week' (a British National Savings campaign in which the civilian community raised money for equipment for the army; the RAF equivalent was 'Wings for Victory' and the Royal Navy's 'Warship Week'), the Lord Mayor of London, Sir Frank Newson-Smith, gave a banquet at Mansion House. Newspapers reported that among the distinguished guests was Sir Bernard Montgomery, 'on his first official visit to the city since he became commander of the British Forces for the invasion of Europe'.

The Ministry of Fuel and Power was already running a newspaper advertisement campaign in which it implored citizens to sacrifice their comfort to save more 'Fuel for the Battle':

'Yours is a heavy responsibility if you have a gas or an electric fire, for every time you enjoy its warmth you are eating into the coal supplies – coal needed for the invasion of Europe, the most vital military operation in history. Think twice before you light that fire. Realise that you are tapping the sources of victory and – tap sparingly. Fires? Yes, and ovens, hot water, and lighting too – the country is relying on the willing co-operation and deep sense of responsibility of its citizens for the saving of the fuel for all these. Careless use of gas or electricity at this moment of the war is a shameful thing.'

Even the Nazis' own newspaper, *Völkischer Beobachter*, warned the German people about the coming Allied entry into Europe and that 'a large-scale invasion will be carried out with ruthless energy by the Allies and with great superiority in men and material'. Not only was the invasion now accepted as a certainty by the Nazis, so too was the fact that the liberating troops would be coming to stay. Hitler's newspaper did not promise that within a few hours the invading forces would be swept into the sea. Instead, it admitted that 'fierce fighting will occur in the fortified zones and also in the regions behind'. The reasons given were 'that the Allies want to force a decision on the Germans' and that 'therefore they will throw in all they have got and not be scared by initial failures'. *Völkischer Beobachter* also made a remarkable, if casual, reference to the Russian campaign and to a possible Soviet triumph. 'Developments in recent weeks,' it said, 'have forced Britain and the US to bite the hard nut of invasion, otherwise the Western Powers might come too late on the field and will find Stalin sole victor on the European battlefield.'

There was a newspaper published in London that was regularly delivered to Berlin and other German cities being carpet-bombed by the Allies. The four-page *Sternenbanner* ('Star-spangled Banner') was dropped after the bombers had delivered their lethal load. The newspaper was printed in German, Dutch, French and Flemish, on special lightweight paper so that it could be passed from hand to hand inside occupied territories.

The *Daily Mirror* reported, 'It is telling the truth about the progress of the mighty Allied air assault on enslaved Europe, about the failure of the U-boat campaign … Himmler has decreed twenty years' imprisonment as the lowest penalty for reading it and threatens the death penalty in severe cases.'

One night in April, people in the English Midlands thought that the invasion had begun when a huge air convoy created an impressive spectacle as the green and red navigation lights of both gliders and transport planes made a brilliant pattern in the night sky. That was a false dawn, but, as invasion day grew ever nearer, the significance of this truly awesome adventure came home

D-Day to VE Day

D-Day to VE Day

The Final Year of the War in Europe

Anton Rippon and
Nicola Rippon

PEN & SWORD
HISTORY

First published in Great Britain in 2024 by
Pen & Sword History
An imprint of Pen & Sword Books Limited
Yorkshire – Philadelphia

Copyright © Anton Rippon and Nicola Rippon 2024

ISBN 978 1 39905 621 2

The rights of Anton Rippon and Nicola Rippon to be identified as
Authors of this Work has been asserted by them in accordance
with the Copyright, Designs and Patents Act 1988.

A CIP catalogue record for this book is
available from the British Library

All rights reserved. No part of this book may be reproduced or
transmitted in any form or by any means, electronic or mechanical
including photocopying, recording or by any information storage and
retrieval system, without permission from the Publisher in writing.

Typeset by Mac Style
Printed in the UK by CPI Group (UK) Ltd, Croydon, CR0 4YY.

MIX
Paper | Supporting
responsible forestry
FSC
www.fsc.org   FSC® C013604

Pen & Sword Books Limited incorporates the imprints of After
the Battle, Atlas, Archaeology, Aviation, Discovery, Family History,
Fiction, History, Maritime, Military, Military Classics, Politics,
Select, Transport, True Crime, Air World, Frontline Publishing, Leo
Cooper, Remember When, Seaforth Publishing, The Praetorian Press,
Wharncliffe Local History, Wharncliffe Transport, Wharncliffe True
Crime and White Owl.

For a complete list of Pen & Sword titles please contact

PEN & SWORD BOOKS LIMITED
47 Church Street, Barnsley, South Yorkshire, S70 2AS, England
E-mail: enquiries@pen-and-sword.co.uk
Website: www.pen-and-sword.co.uk
or
PEN AND SWORD BOOKS
1950 Lawrence Rd, Havertown, PA 19083, USA
E-mail: uspen-and-sword@casematepublishers.com
Website: www.penandswordbooks.com

This book is dedicated to the war correspondents who went into the battle armed only with their pens and notebooks.

Contents

Prelude

Four years ago our nation and empire stood alone against an overwhelming enemy, with our backs to the wall ... Now once more a supreme test has to be faced ...

King George VI

Just before 8.40pm on 22 January 1944, air-raid warning sirens wailed out over London. Shortly afterwards, more than 400 German bombers arrived over the capital. Westminster was soon in flames as large numbers of incendiary bombs fell around Parliament. The Embankment and New Scotland Yard were among other sites hit. Just before dawn broke, another wave of bombers arrived and, by daybreak, almost 100 Londoners lay dead, and hundreds more were in hospital. The Luftwaffe's Operation Steinbock had begun.

It was a shock. The alert, followed by the drone of approaching Dorniers, Heinkels and Junkers, were sounds that most people in Britain thought they had heard for the last time. At the height of the Blitz, between September 1940 and May 1941, more than 43,000 civilians had been killed in air raids on Britain's towns and cities. Half of those perished in London. Militarily, however, the Blitz was a failure, and it came to an end as Hitler prepared to invade the Soviet Union – his Operation Barbarossa – in June 1941. For two and a half years thereafter, occasional raids on Britain were carried out by small numbers of bombers, but there was nothing on the scale of the Blitz and, as the balance of the war altered, it was the Allies' pounding of German cities that began to capture newspaper headlines. Now, in a raid as large and heavy as any previous attack, the 'Baby Blitz', as British newspapers called Operation Steinbock, catapulted Londoners back to those nights of terror of three years earlier.

Whatever its name, it was the start of a four-month onslaught, the final German bombing offensive of the Second World War. Originally targeted at Southern England, in March Operation Steinbock was extended to the North, and cities such as Hull and Manchester were given a grim reminder – if one was needed – of the heavy bombing suffered during 1941. Bristol was also fully to everyone, whether they were the men and women working long shifts to produce munitions, those passing time in the pub – when beer was available – or housewives chatting in the corner shop as they queued up to collect the weekly food ration.

People asked themselves: if it succeeded, then surely it would herald, if not the end, then at least the beginning of the end, of all the pain and suffering that Adolf Hitler had heaped upon the world since 1939. Loved ones could come home, and, as for the future ... well, as uncertain as it might look, at least there would be a future. But what if it failed? Apart from the obvious military disaster, a weary nation began to wonder if it would have the energy to begin all over again. Unlike the First World War, no-one had thought in 1939 that, this time, it really would be 'all over by Christmas'. But this war had already lasted for five years. And, unlike the First World War, when the battles raged across the sea, this time almost every home in Britain had been on the front line at one time or another. The nation was exhausted.

The news kept coming. But when would the invasion begin? On 5 June, there were reports that between 500 to 750 Eighth Air Force Fortresses and Liberators, with an escort of up to 500 fighters, had attacked German military installations on the coast of Northern France, which, together with Cologne, had been the target of the RAF a few hours earlier. The first formations had flown over the English coast at dawn, and witnesses said that they could hear bombs exploding and anti-aircraft guns firing on the other side of the Channel. Thunderbolt fighter-bombers, escorted by Marauders, attacked anti-aircraft defences, and rocket-carrying Typhoons targeted radio installations. According to reports, the operation, which included mine-laying, had been accomplished without the loss of a single Allied aircraft.

One reporter telephoned that formations of Allied heavy bombers were passing out over the East Anglian coast 'in almost continuous procession'. The air armada had begun soon after dawn, and, five hours later, planes were still heading out over the North Sea.

In late May, Joseph Goebbels, the Nazis' chief propagandist, writing in the weekly newspaper that he had founded, *Das Reich*, under the heading 'The Greatest Test', had warned, 'The war has reached its greatest climax and the great crisis is approaching. Political manoeuvres will not bring the war to an end. It is not true that we are placing all our troops on dissension in the Allied camp. We realise that this war will be decided on the battlefield. We must consider it as a certainty that the Allies will invade.'

Now, as D-Day drew near, the impending invasion was affecting all manner of things in Britain. The National Fire Service cricket team had 'found it necessary' to cancel their matches scheduled for Bath and Nottingham that week, and the committee of Tattersalls was having to hold an emergency meeting to decide, in the event of the 1944 Derby and The Oaks either being postponed to a future date or abandoned altogether, what should be done about ante-post betting. Filmgoers, meanwhile, could choose from a large selection of films being shown at the nation's many cinemas, including *Hitler's Madman*, a highly fictionalised account of the 1942 assassination of Nazi official Reinhard Heydrich and the resultant Lidice massacre committed by the Nazis in revenge. For those who preferred lighter viewing there was always the American musical *What's Buzzin', Cousin?* The BBC's radio schedule for 5 June 1944 included, on the Home Service, *Music While You Work* and 'a talk on milk', while the General Forces Programme's offerings included *Variety Bandbox*, *Sports Gazette* and *Voice of the Violin*.

Whatever their choice of entertainment, the British people went to bed that night with a sense of great events impending. They knew that any day now would come the news of the battle that would alter the course of their lives, and the lives of their children and their grandchildren, forever.

The following day's morning newspapers and early morning radio news bulletins were full of the fall of Rome to the Allies, which had been announced the day before. At times the Italian campaign had been a brutal one as the Allies made the heavy slog up the boot of Italy. The weather had been terrible – cold, rain and mud through the autumn, winter and early spring of 1943–44. Only after the Allies broke out of Cassino and Anzio, took Rome and went slowly on to Florence and the Apennines were the troops able to enjoy something of the glorious summer of 1944, the war in Italy all but won.

At 9.33am on 6 June 1944 came the brief announcement from Supreme HQ Allied Expeditionary Force (SHAEF): 'Under the command of General Eisenhower, Allied naval forces, supported by strong air forces, began landing Allied armies this morning on the coast of France.' D-Day had dawned.

Chapter 1

D-Day – 6 June 1944

Good luck to each one of you. And good hunting on the mainland of Europe.
General Bernard Montgomery

'Our Armies in Northern France ... Deliverance Day has dawned' – the front page of the *Hull Daily Mail* was typical of Britain's evening newspapers for 6 June 1944. The great Allied invasion for the liberation of Europe had begun early that morning with landings on Normandy beaches.

Already British and Canadian forces had secured at least two beachhead points, reports said, and, in Parliament, Prime Minister Winston Churchill told the House of Commons, 'An immense armada of upwards of 4,000 ships, with several thousand smaller craft, have crossed the Channel.' Massed airborne landings had been successfully effected behind the enemy's lines, he said, and the invasion was supported by 11,000 front-line aircraft from the RAF and USAF, and so far the commanders who were engaged reported that everything was proceeding as planned. Asked if he would keep the House fully informed, Churchill said, 'It may be that I shall ask their indulgence to press myself upon them before we rise tonight.'

Ironically, the very first reports of the invasion had come, not from the Allies but from the German Overseas News Agency:

'Early this morning numerous landing craft and light warships were observed in the area between the mouth of the Seine and the eastern coast of Normandy. At the same time paratroops were dropped from numerous aircraft on the northern tip of the Normandy peninsula. It is believed that these paratroops have been given the task of capturing airfields in order to facilitate the landing of further paratroops. The harbour of Le Havre is at the moment being bombarded. German naval forces have engaged enemy craft off the coast. The long expected invasion appears to have begun.'

One German military commentator, Captain Ludwig Sertorius, welcomed it:

'The German soldiers have always wished the invasion to come so that they could show their moral supremacy in a fight not marked by material inferiority such as was the case in Africa and Italy ... They are coming, and it is good that they should come.'

While the German Overseas News Agency continued to give regular updates, the German people were not told of the landings in that morning's early bulletins of the domestic radio service. 'Germany clear of raiders' they were assured. The overseas service, however, pressed on with the bad news: its military correspondent, Lieutenant Colonel Alfred von Olberg, who was recognised as one of Germany's foremost commentators, was in no mood to keep the momentous events from the world at large, although, in 1915, as head of the War Press Office in Berlin, he had subscribed to the view that 'the accuracy of the message is less important that its effect', and now suggested that the invasion might not be the real thing:

'D-Day has dawned – the invasion has begun. The tension which held the whole of Europe in its grip during the past week begins to relax. With the Allied landing attempt in Northern France, the second front or, better the third front, has come into being. It remains to be seen whether this landing attempt marks the beginning of the great invasion. It is quite possible that the enemy is planning a feint, or else are a holding attack in order to deceive the German High Command to cause premature German troop movements.'

While German press and radio wrestled with how best to present news of the Allied invasion, British newspapers were gung-ho with tales of 'Allied bombers roaring overhead at dawn to give the British people the first hint that big events were under way'. The BBC's French language transmission began to warn French people to get away from coastal areas and to avoid roads, railways and bridges. Agency reports said,

'So, little more than four years after the remnants of the British army, battle-stained and weary, were snatched from destruction at Dunkirk, they returned to Europe ten times more numerous, armed with the weapons they then lacked, and with the knowledge of a glorious record of North Africa and Italy to sustain them. Plans had been made to the last detail for one of the greatest events in history. The men had been trained to the last ounce, skilled in the use of the most modern weapons, and hardened like fine steel.'

Plans for an Allied force to liberate Occupied Europe had been drawn up as long ago as September 1941, when discussions, codenamed Operation Roundup, began to look at a possible invasion of Northern France in the spring of 1943. A shortage of equipment, particularly of landing craft, rendered that unrealistic. Churchill, meanwhile, preferred to attack 'the soft underbelly of Europe' by invading from the Mediterranean Sea. But, eventually, through plans like Operation Sledgehammer and Operation Roundhammer (an improved version of Roundup) and something called Skyscraper, what was now Operation Overlord evolved. Eisenhower was to be the supreme commander. Commander of overall Allied ground operations would be General Bernard Montgomery, commander of the victorious Eighth Army in North Africa and during the invasion of Sicily and the 'toe' of Italy, where he had clashed with American generals George Patton and Omar Bradley over tactics.

Many things had made D-Day possible, including the Allies' bombing campaign that began in 1942. German industry was weakened, and German troops were drawn away from the French coast to concentrate on home defence. Allied air superiority over the landing grounds was also essential. However, perhaps the most important factor in the success of Overlord would be the deception tactics that saw the German High Command continually having to adjust their plans. Where would the Allies land their forces? The Pas-de-Calais across the Strait of Dover seemed the obvious answer, and the Allies did their best to encourage that belief. While the royal family's regular visits around the country had helped maintain public morale, they were also used to shore up the war effort more directly. As preparations for the Allied invasion of France began, the King, Queen and Princess Elizabeth made several highly publicised visits to troops stationed in the South-East. When the monarch also visited a huge oil-storage complex near Dover, at the narrowest point of the English Channel, it seemed to suggest that action was imminent and that an attack point near Calais had been chosen. But things were not what they seemed. The oil depot was actually an elaborate fake designed by architect Basil Spence and built by Shepperton Studios on behalf of the War Office. Messages intercepted at Bletchley Park showed that the royals' participation in the deception had been key in convincing Hitler that the first landings would be at Calais. By the time the Führer realised his mistake, the largest amphibious invasion in history was well under way elsewhere. The target was five beaches near Caen, west of the River Orne, codenamed Sword, Juno, Gold, Omaha and Utah. Stormy weather in the Channel threatened the operation, but a slight improvement in conditions, which allowed Allied airpower to play its part, brought the irrevocable decision to launch Overlord on 6 June, although the still heavy, pitching sea would make it a harrowing experience for many.

That day, the British would land 67,715 troops, including 177 French commandos, plus airborne, on Gold and Sword; the Americans 73,000, plus airborne, on Utah and Omaha; the Canadians 21,400 on Juno. Almost 7,000 naval vessels – 4,000 of them landing craft – and 95,000 naval personnel were involved, and the landings were supported by 11,500 aircraft flying 14,000 sorties. The day ended with heavy casualties – 4,414 Allied soldiers killed and more than 6,000 wounded in the first twenty-four hours. German casualties on D-Day were estimated at between 4,000 and 9,000, either killed, wounded or missing. The Allies had established a foothold. All the troops had been landed, and those on the flanks had already contacted airborne units. The advance into France could begin.

The naval vessels were taking part in Operation Neptune, which was the escorting and landing component of Overlord. They also carried out bombardments of German coastal defences and provided artillery support for the invading troops. Among them was 20-year-old Gerald Mumby, who had been working at an Inland Revenue Office in Derby before being called up to join the Royal Navy. In June 1943, he reported to HMS *Royal Arthur*, a shore base at Butlin's, Skegness. It was the beginning of a great adventure because he was one of the first ashore on D-Day.

'I was serving as a naval telegraphist. I landed at 8.30am, on Gold Beach with a forward observation bombardment unit. There were three of us in an armoured 9-tonne [9,144kg] half-track: me, an artillery officer, and an artillery bombardier, who was the driver.

'The officer would work out where he wanted our ships offshore to aim their shells, then I would relay the bearings to the ships. I was lucky because our bit of the beach was relatively quiet; there were only a few bodies about. But of the 100 FOB [Forward Operating Base] units that went ashore, only thirty returned.

'As we were preparing to drive ashore off the landing craft, the jeep in front went straight down into the sea and sank. Then we couldn't get through because the sand dunes had been mined and we had to wait for them to be cleared. We were on the beach until about 11am, then we could move inland.'

For people back home, Combined Press correspondents painted the picture. From the bridge of a destroyer some 4.5 miles [7.3km] off Berniere-sur-Mer, 7 miles [11.2km] east of Arromanches, Desmond Tighe of Reuters could see 'rolling clouds of dense black and grey smoke covered the beaches south-west of Le Havre'. He wrote, 'I can see vast numbers of naval craft. In ten minutes more than 2,000 tons [1814.3 tonnes] of HE shells have gone down on the beachhead. It is now exactly 7.26am … through my glasses I can see the first wave of assault troops touching down on the water's edge and fan up the beach.'

Associated Press journalist Gladwin Hill had a grandstand aerial view from the cockpit of a Marauder medium bomber that took part in the first bombardment that morning:

'I saw great naval and shore engagements getting under way. A few miles inland I saw fields strewn with hundreds of parachutes where Allied airborne forces had dropped. The fields were dotted, too, with aircraft, probably gliders, bearing the distinctive Allied invasion black and white zebra stripe which was hurriedly slapped on the aircraft late yesterday.'

Alfred C. Fletcher reported, 'The naval people that I have spoken to so far are very pleased with the results. They consider that the Germans were taken completely off their guard by believing that the invasion could only take place in the calmest of weather.'

Tom Yarborough: 'The Germans didn't pull any radically new or "secret" weapons. When the crew of this ship was told an assault will be made on the coast of France there was a moment of utter silence. Then a babble of exclamation swept the room – something like a great sigh of relief. One of the youngest lads said, "I'm from Coventry and I've got something to fight for".'

William Stewart: 'At 5am, an officer reported, "Dawn's pink hand is delicately brushing the sky up, and we can see the reflection of our bombing explosions on Jerry." Three or four officers then sat down to breakfast calmly. They had cereal, liver, bacon and browned potatoes, bread and butter, marmalade and piping hot coffee.' W.R. Higginbotham: 'American invasion troops were made ready financially for the assault on France with a payday in franc notes, some dated in 1944 and bearing the authority of the Bank of France … The invasion began when bombers hit a 2,000-yard [1.81km] strip of beach. Flares lit the night, and inside the flare paths, flashes of light, followed by great roars of bombs and bursts of ack-ack fire, told of dead-centre aiming. A similar bombardment followed on another beach. On a long stretch of beach, other bombs did their deadly work on gun emplacements and, between beachheads, a battery of French 155mm weapons manned by the Germans took a powerful thumping.'

An unnamed correspondent wrote: 'From the cockpit of one of the many hundreds of planes which supported the Allied landing early this morning, I watched the battle royal rage on sea and in the air. The fields along the French Channel coast were dotted with parachutes of the Allied airborne forces who had landed a few minutes before, and interspersed among the parachutes were aircraft, probably gliders. The first signs of battle were flashes from the Channel below which, through the mist and naval smokescreen, gradually became distinguishable as gun detonations of warships shelling coast. The Channel was not jammed with shipping as one might have expected, but on every hand were forces of ships either battering the coastline or bringing up forces to take advantage of breaches.'

Back across the Channel, the first evening newspapers were eagerly snapped up, and queues formed at street stands, waiting for the next edition even before it came off the press. In London, a nurse, who was helping at a stand for Red Cross Flag Day, said, 'What a relief it's been. Like waiting for a thunderstorm to burst.' A woman came up and the nurse handed her an emblem. 'No,' she said. 'I want more than one. I want several. My son is a prisoner. What is happening today will bring him home sooner.' In a nearby milk bar, two NFS men toasted the invasion in tea. 'You can fight fires better on this stuff,' said one. 'Jerry may not take it lying down.' In St Paul's Cathedral, a small service was being held, and a hymn was sung, unaccompanied except for the drone of aircraft overhead.

King George VI had spoken to the nation many times during the war. During the most difficult days, it had been the king's speeches to his people that had provided the greatest morale boosts. Unlike his prime minister, George VI was a far from confident orator. Nevertheless, his words had always hit the right tone. At the very start of the war, he had spoken of determination and dedication to protect the 'sake of all that we ourselves hold dear and of the world order and peace'. In particular, his Christmas Day messages had offered reassurance to listeners around the world. In that first Christmas message of the war, he had talked of a 'family of nations which is prepared to sacrifice everything that freedom of spirit may be saved to the world'. In 1940, he recognised the difficulties of separation from loved ones, and of the unity that facing a common threat had brought. The message of 1941 remembered 'the men who in every part of the world are serving the Empire and its cause with such valour and devotion by sea, land and in the air', the women 'who at the call of duty have left their homes to join the services, or to work in factory, hospital or field' and also those who were bereaved, wounded or imprisoned by the enemy. In 1942, he recognised the contribution of the United States and the Soviet Union, as well as the people of India as they faced the threat of invasion by Japan. As ever, the king recognised the work of people on the

Home Front, paying particular thanks to those working the land. In 1943, he highlighted the spirit of the people who 'know that much hard working, and hard fighting – perhaps harder working and harder fighting than ever before – are necessary for victory. We shall not rest from our task until it is nobly ended.'

His words on D-Day were as memorable as any. Coming at the end of a long day, during which Britons had tuned into each news broadcast, desperately awaiting the latest invasion report, by the time the monarch spoke he had, according to newspaper reports the next day, 'the biggest radio audience in history'. Speaking in his slow and careful way, each word deliberately pronounced, he said that, from the very start of the conflict, 'the spirit of the people, resolute, dedicated, burned like a bright flame, lit surely from those unseen fires which nothing can quench'. He told his people,

'Now once more a supreme test has to be faced. This time, the challenge is not to fight to survive but to fight to win the final victory for the good cause. Once again what is demanded from us all is something more than courage and endurance; we need a revival of spirit, a new unconquerable resolve' and so he called his people 'to prayer and dedication. We are not unmindful of our own shortcomings, past and present. We shall ask not that God may do our will, but that we may be enabled to do the will of God ...'

On Friday, 16 June, just ten days after D-Day, King George VI visited the Normandy beachheads. He crossed the Channel aboard the light cruiser HMS *Arethusa*, making the final trip to shore on an amphibious 'duck'. As the king jumped nimbly from the craft, he was greeted by the waiting General Montgomery in full battledress.

'Good Morning, Your Majesty. Welcome to France!' said the general as he and his monarch shook hands. All around them, dozens more landing craft, bearing troops, tanks and munitions, were arriving in what a *Daily Telegraph* correspondent called an 'endless stream of convoys and craft of every kind going to and from the beachhead'.

All the while, six-inch shells from the heavy cruiser HMS *Hawkins* flew overhead, bound for a target some 10 miles (16km) inland. The pair lunched at Monty's advanced HQ at Creully, 4 miles (6.4km) from the Normandy beaches, before the king performed an open-air investiture. Only 6 miles (9.6km) from the front, he decorated, among others, Major General Rodney Keller, commander of the Canadian 3rd Division, with the CBE.

That it was deemed safe enough for the king to spend three hours in France – albeit with the escort of two destroyers, and overhead Spitfire cover – said much about the early successes of Operation Overlord. And it left a great impact on the king who, later that day, sent a message to General Eisenhower:

'Today I have visited the beaches of Normandy, which will be forever famous. All that I saw on my journey, and on the soils of France, has moved me deeply. I have come home feeling an intense admiration for all those who planned and organised so vast a project and for the gallant and successful execution of it in all its various phases by every one of those now engaged in this great battle.'

The Normandy beachheads had hardly been established when people at home began to see something of the other side of the picture. On 13 June, only a week after D-Day, the first convoy of wounded soldiers arrived at English railway stations. A grim procession of stretchers carried casualties from trains to the waiting ambulances. Men in hospital blue became a familiar sight in many towns and cities. The Battle of Normandy would be about more than just D-Day.

In Ramsgate, the Sherred family received a letter from their son, Corporal Elgar Sherred, who wrote from a military hospital in southern England: '... It is nothing much – only a bullet through my foot. Don't worry ... I didn't stop very long did I?'

From one unnamed British port, war reporter John Marshall told of 'lines of ambulances threading through the docks, waiting for the hospital ships which arrived at regular intervals now'.

The *Aberdeen Press and Journal's* John Allan Graydon reported that air transport had reduced the death rate: '... Relatives in Britain, knowing that their husbands, fathers and sons are at this moment fighting in France, will be pleased to hear that everything possible is being done to make sure that the wounded are given speedy attention. Already some of those suffering from wounds have returned; proof that speed is the keynote of our medical services' work. As a direct result of the use of air transport for removing wounded from "battlefield hospitals" to the peace and quiet of a British hospital, the death rate, in some cases, has been reduced to 5 in 1,500 severely wounded men. In France during the last war, the figure was 130.

'In past campaigns head wounds were a source of worry to the medical services, and unless a soldier suffering from an injury of this kind was rushed to a base hospital and given the finest treatment, he usually died. In North Africa, however, because air ambulances were used so effectively, only one-tenth of the men suffering from head wounds failed to survive ... Sometimes, in emergency, doctors have been known, when travelling through the air at 200mph, to perform little "miracles" that have saved a man's life.'

Fred Perfect, the *Daily Telegraph*'s special naval war correspondent, told how a tank-landing ship had left for Normandy two days earlier with her lower and upper decks packed with tanks, and how she was now returning to England as 'a hospital ship with every facility on board for the care of wounded men'.

The organisation for the removal and treatment of casualties was truly impressive, said Perfect. Long before the first assault parties had landed on invasion morning, places ashore had been mapped out for use as first-aid posts, clearing stations and field hospitals. Within an hour or two of the initial assault, captured German pillboxes were flying the Red Cross and dealing with their first wounded.

An RAMC officer showed Perfect around: 'Aft, the ship carries a removable operating theatre equipped with everything that might be required on the passage. Each ship carries tubes of penicillin, and I saw several blood transfusions being given.

> 'In the hold, the less seriously wounded men were enjoying a last smoke before settling down for the crossing. Not one of them had been wounded earlier than two days ago – striking evidence of the celerity with which they were embarked.'

A burly Northumbrian grumbled because he had been wounded by a shell before he had left the beach. The first Germans he saw were a group of wounded prisoners among his fellow-passengers. 'I did reckon to get one Jerry before going down,' he said.

Private Ernest Simpson of Fife told Perfect, 'It was really peculiar how I was wounded. Somebody had dug a slit trench which must have been right alongside a booby trap. I put my right hand up to the parapet to jump out and – up it went.'

Many of the wounded men spoke of booby traps and snipers. 'There were Jerry hand-grenades lying about all over place,' said Private Simpson. 'Some were wired to mines under the soil, some had trip-wires, and some were made to go off the moment you cut the wire.'

Private Alan Miller of East Ham, who had been in the fighting east of the Orne, said, 'We had heard a lot about the German mortars, but for two or three days we saw nothing of them. I suppose we had begun to forget them, for I was standing in the open when suddenly down came a mortar bomb – and here I am.'

Many of the wounded asked Perfect if they had an escort across the Channel: 'I assured them that the Navy was shepherding them home and with that they turned contentedly to sleep.'

Chapter 2

The Gates of Hell

I suppose that when the Germans get through the gap ... they imagine that they have escaped. But the bigger and more terrible picture for them is now taking shape.

Alexander Clifford, Sunday Despatch

That the Allies had, on the very first day of Operation Overlord, established a firm beachhead was due in no small part to some inventive pieces of engineering. Inside those first twenty-four hours, as well as men, vehicles and supplies had also been brought ashore. Fuel was delivered to the coast of Normandy from storage tanks on the south coast of England by means of PLUTO (Pipeline Under The Ocean), submarine oil pipelines laid under the English Channel that reduced the need for tankers that would be a target for the Luftwaffe. And, until they could capture a major harbour, the Allies relied on two floating harbours that were built in seventy-three separate sections, towed across the Channel and assembled precisely where they would be used.

On Gold Beach, the British and Canadians used Mulberry 'B', which, for the next ten months, saw 2.5 million men, 500,000 vehicles and 4 million tonnes of supplies unloaded for the push into North-West Europe. Mulberry 'A' supplied the Americans at Omaha Beach until it was broken up by a storm that blew in on 19 June. Some structural elements of Mulberry 'A' were then used to extend Mulberry 'B', or 'Port Winston' as it was nicknamed by British and Canadian troops.

In the hedgerow country of Normandy, progress was slow but, by late June, with their complete air superiority, more troops and far greater resources, the Allies had captured the port of Cherbourg. On 24 June, the German News Agency reported that, after several hours of bitter fighting, the Americans had succeeded in penetrating the south and south-eastern sectors of the outer Cherbourg defence belt in three places, and then employed their heaviest guns to pave the way for further thrusts. 'Subsequent efforts to break into Cherbourg city proper were beaten back in bloody fighting,' added the agency. Two days later, however, Cherbourg was in Americans hands and, by September, it was the major port through which US supplies went for the remainder of the war.

The British 3rd Infantry Division was supposed to seize Caen – 10 miles (16km) from the coast, at the mouth of the River Orne – on D-Day itself, but it was not captured until July, after a massive British-Canadian armoured attack that was met with fierce resistance. On 21 August, General Miles Dempsey, commander of the British 2nd Army, presented a gold sword and plaque to the mayor of Caen, saying, 'We share your grief at the scars which mark your historic city; we extend our sympathy to your bereaved; but we rejoice that the spirit of Caen has remained unbroken by these heavy trials.'

Newspapermen embedded with the Allied forces described the difficult, often harrowing conditions faced by the troops. 'Normandy,' wrote Press Association correspondent William E. West, 'is the only place I know where it can rain and still stay dusty.' 'There is dust everywhere,' reported West. 'It follows every jeep and truck in clouds, and shrouds the hedgerows on the fields, settles in the eyes, hair and throat. It comes from the vast airfields being built in the American sector and from the great excavators which are ruthlessly widening the narrow Normandy lanes … The main roads so crowded with military traffic are reminiscent of the Brighton road on a summer Sunday, though the American military police were not perhaps so long-suffering and patient as our traffic control officers.' Damage varied enormously, said West. The centre of one small town was a scene of indescribable havoc, yet only a couple of hundred yards away, a villa looked unscathed 'with pretty curtains behind polished windows'.

Yorkshire Post war correspondent Joe Illingworth reported from Sannerville, a village south of the four jump zones planned by the 6th Airborne Division for the eve of D-Day, and from where all the remaining inhabitants had been evacuated five days before the commencement of the controversial Operation Goodwood, in which Montgomery planned to somehow squeeze three armoured divisions across a small bridgehead over the Orne.

A massive bombardment had destroyed Sannerville's 133 dwellings before the 3rd Royal Tank Regiment captured what was now a heap of rubble. Illingworth wrote, 'The last of the Germans who survived our air bombardment of Sannerville on Tuesday morning were mopped up in its ruins last night. Those who were killed by our bombs lie in the blasted orchards between Sannerville and Touffreville.'

Illingworth had approached Sannerville through Touffreville: 'I shall always remember that because the end of Touffreville's one street had that sickly sweet smell which tells you that there are dead men about. They were in the rubble which is Touffreville, and they were in those orchards. The orchards had been so pounded that no green showed in them. The rich, red brown earth of Normandy lay deep under slabs of grey clay, and the dead sprawled on the clay.'

Private John Clark of City Walk, Pendlebury, Manchester, told Illingworth that there were eleven dead Germans in a gun-pit, but the journalist could see only seven. There was a lot of water in the pit and the other four were under it. The seven that Illingworth could see were all huddled together on the sloping side of the gun-pit: 'They may have been old or they may have been young. You could not tell ... They were all covering their eyes with their hands and arms or were pressing their faces against the earth. It was an awful sight. They had seen death coming to them from the skies and they had tried to shut it out.

'They had tried to shut it out as the citizens of Rotterdam had tried to shut it out a long time ago, when the Luftwaffe held the skies; as the citizens of Hull and Liverpool, and Belfast and Coventry had tried, and as the citizens of London try now ... There was another dead German in a ditch just beyond the gun-pit. And he, too, was covering his eyes with his arm. One of his boots had been torn off. You always notice the boots of a dead man ...'

Montgomery's plan proved costly – the Allies lost 400 tanks destroyed or abandoned, and more than 4,000 men in Operation Goodwood – but the distraction had allowed the Americans, in Patton's Operation Cobra, to make progress around the town of Avranches, which stood on high ground and represented, across the Pontaubault Bridge that spanned the River Selune, the gateway into Brittany. Again, the Americans suffered heavy casualties, not least at the hands of their own bombers whose crews were confused by bad weather and the close proximity of their own troops during the largest carpet bombing operation of the war. Overall, Operation Cobra cost more than 5,000 American lives but, in terms of its objective, it was an overwhelming success.

On 16 August, the day after American and French forces landed in Provence for the invasion of southern France, Hitler gave the order to withdraw from Normandy. The Battle of the Falaise Pocket – a 15-mile (25km) wide gap between the towns of Falaise and Argentan in the Calvados region – was to prove the decisive action of the Normandy campaign. British, American, Canadian and Polish troops had all but encircled more than 100,000 German soldiers. It is estimated that between 20,000 and 50,000 managed to escape, leaving behind all their equipment, that between 10,000 to 15,000 were either killed or wounded, some 40,000 to 50,000 were captured, and 500 German tanks and artillery pieces were destroyed. Estimates vary wildly, depending on what case is being made; one calculation has 270,000 Germans either in the

Falaise Pocket or heading towards the Seine, and that as many as 210,000 of them escaped through the gap.

William Wilson, a British United Press correspondent with the Canadian army, reported on some of those taken prisoner: 'Some were trudging wearily along on foot; others were driving their own vehicles crammed with loot that they had taken from the French and, believe it or not, they wanted to take this loot with them to the prison cages.'

Wilson told the story of an SS officer taken prisoner: 'He was manning a machine gun behind seven ordinary infantrymen. He barked out the orders and told them to fight on to the end, but he surrendered quickly enough when the Canadians got near. We told him to stand against the wall, and his veil of arrogance disappeared like smoke in the wind. His knees shook and his lips trembled. He thought we were going to shoot him. Then he burst into tears, pleading pitifully to the Canadians not to shoot him. The Canadians laughed and sent the weeping superman off to the prison cage.

'We had another weeping prisoner, but the tears were not so out of place this time, for the prisoner was a woman. She had been sniping for the Germans. She said she was a Russian who had been captured on the Briansk Front in Russia and brought to France by her captors. Strangest of all were the twenty Mongolians. By some freak of war, they found themselves manning German machine-guns and killing Canadians. But there are some Germans who never change their colour. We found one car which contained loot stolen from French houses. It had everything, from wireless sets to knives and forks.'

Alexander Clifford, a reporter with the British forces, described the scene at what he called 'the Gates of Hell' as troops of the German 7th Army fled:

'All through the night the gap was hideous with livid flames from burning transport. A burning lorry makes a big and lasting blaze. There were hundreds of them. The sun had scarcely risen yesterday morning when our first planes came tearing out of the soft white clouds of a summer sky. The traffic jam was still there, everything that could move was still dragging itself east. Then the carnage began again. Trucks are nose-to-tail in every road and lane. Then a vehicle is shot into flames. The lane can't be used until the vehicle is burnt out. There is no room to pass … there is no shape or order anymore, everywhere confusion.'

The Reuters special correspondent with the Canadians wrote,

'An eerie quiet hung over Falaise as I stood on a hilltop and looked over the corridor which is the only escape route for nobody knows how many thousands of the German Seventh Army. The Americans, just few miles away, were driving up from Argentan to meet us. I had expected at least plenty of gunfire with the Germans trying to force a passage while they could, but during two hours in Falaise I did not hear one artillery piece, either German or our own. If the Germans realise they are trapped, they are certainly taking it very calmly. The only firing came from snipers who still infest Falaise and from parties of Canadian infantrymen hunting them.

'Looking out over the woods and wheatfields known as the Falaise Gap we could see no movement. The road from Caen to Falaise gave a picture of the kind of fighting the Canadians had over this 20-mile [32km] stretch of rolling farmland and orchard. Wrecked vehicles – most of them German – littered the road. Alongside roads were knocked-out Tiger tanks, monsters which apparently had exploded from one shell hit from our 17-pounders. The last stretch, which had been in our hands only a few hours, was covered with tree branches and other debris amid which the Engineers were at work, clearing mines. The last 100yd [91m] to Falaise is downhill and from the top one gets a panoramic view of the city in the valley below. The wreckage is not as bad as in the worst part of Caen or Saint-Lô, but it is impossible for anybody to live in it.' At the crossroads in the centre of the town, the Reuters man met the colonel of the first tank regiment to enter Falaise. 'In Caen we were up against the SS boys, and it was fierce fighting,' he said. 'Here it was just ordinary German infantrymen – duck soup.'

In the narrow lanes and minor roads that were the Germans' only escape route, and in the fields that surrounded them, the smell of death was everywhere. Corpses of soldiers and civilians, along with those of thousands of cattle and horses, lay across a huge area, every one of them covered in maggots and flies in the hot August sun. Eisenhower later wrote,

'The battlefield at Falaise was unquestionably one of the greatest "killing fields" of any of the war areas. Forty-eight hours after the closing of the gap I was conducted through it on foot, to encounter scenes that could be described only by Dante. It was literally possible to walk for hundreds of yards at a time, stepping on nothing but dead and decaying flesh.'

Many had paid the heaviest price. Argentan had already been bombed by the Allies around D-Day, and the fighting that saw it liberated on 20 August 1944 now left it, quite literally, in ruins.

Squadron Quartermaster Sergeant Peter N. Wood, a former reporter with the *Halifax Evening Courier*, now serving with the British Army, wrote to his old employers, describing his journey through liberated lands:

'It was in the North-West of France, in the industrial areas, where the real spirit of the people began to show itself in the flags and decorations stored up for years and now flying from every house, in the waving and cheering of the children and the aged to every passing vehicle. Every lorry going past was cheered as if it was the Army in itself ...

'They had time, too, to help us by taking on themselves the job of rounding up the odd Germans from their hiding places and of sorting out the traitors in their midst. Here a party of bedraggled Nazis were being marched around the town for all the folk to see them in their plight, and there an angry crowd followed a collaborator being taken off to gaol ...

'...And so it was in all the towns of the last war – Arras, Amiens and so on – towns battered then, damaged in 1940 when the Germans came through, bombed since then by Allies and again battered as the Germans were pushed out. But the people were still going to work and could still turn from stirring amongst the rubble of a home to wave and cheer us on.

'The battle had sped through swiftly and the cemeteries of the last war were untouched, but not uncared for – the hedges were closely trimmed. Flowers lined the graves, and the stone paths were weeded. Here and there, by the wayside, were dotted the graves of this battle, most of them German, with occasionally a wrecked armoured car or vehicle, and a British grave, covered with fresh-cut flowers and neatly enclosed by railings which could only have been erected by the people nearby ...

'You can do nothing wrong. You walk down the street and feel embarrassed as people step off the pavement to let you pass, as they have so long done for the Germans. You feel like a film star as you sign your name in dozens of autograph albums, and give away buttons, badges, cigarettes, sweets and English coins. The gendarmes salute you, everyone wants to shake your hand ... The shops have brought out into their windows everything that has been under the counter, including books banned during the occupation. You are prodded, slapped on the back and greeted effusively in French, Flemish and English.

'The farms give you eggs and fruit. They will take no payment but accept a piece of soap and finger it almost reverently. Soap was four or five shillings a piece (if one could get it) and yet you can buy matches anywhere for a halfpenny a box! There is plenty of beer and cognac, white and red wine, tomatoes, apples, plums in profusion, yet they relish even army biscuits after the brown, sack-tasting bread of four years.

'The trains still run, the cafes are open, the public services are all functioning. But they mourn the burnt-out Palace of Justice and are amazed to learn of the damage in London and the provinces. Each one can tell a story of inspiration, but few do, since to have been in prison, to have a house searched, a husband and son transported to Germany, relatives shot, is the common lot.'

Wood told of two girls who he had met in a restaurant. One was a widow. A month earlier, her husband had been shot for espionage. He was twenty-eight and had been helping British prisoners to reach the frontier, getting information from Germany and passing it back. Before he was shot, he had been tortured, beaten, hung by his manacled wrists. She showed Wood letters from him that had come through underground channels, one written on a piece of clothing. She had herself been imprisoned for nine months. The other girl had helped pilots to escape. She didn't seem to be unduly worried about the danger. It was the risk that many more took.

'For them the war is nearly over,' wrote Wood, 'the battles passed them, and they wait only the return of their menfolk from Germany. Such of them as come back.'

The Battle of the Falaise Pocket brought to an end the Battle for Normandy and opened the road to Paris and, after that, to the borders of a Third Reich teetering on the brink. In late July, the Swiss newspaper, *Journal de Genève*, had reported that the petrol shortage in Germany had assumed disastrous proportions:

'German production is down 35 per cent to 50 per cent, and the shortage of electrical equipment for U-boats is acute. The news that all German women between seventeen and sixty must immediately start working in arms factories is causing apprehension throughout Germany. It is hoped by this means to release between 700,000 and 800,000 men for the services, but official quarters cherish no illusions about the fighting capacity of these recruits, who have never handled a rifle in their lives and who are conscripted at a moment of general depression and flagging morale ...'

Chapter 3

Throes of a Life and Death Crisis

Revolt has broken out in Germany. An attempt has been made by generals to establish a rival government. Hitler has ordered drastic measures to secure his regime.

BBC European service

On 13 March 1943, Fabian von Schlabrendorff, a lawyer by profession and now an adjutant on Adolf Hitler's general staff, ordered a crew member of the aircraft taking Hitler back to Germany from a visit to Army Group Central HQ in Smolensk to deliver a package to a friend. Von Schlabrendorff said that the parcel contained two bottles of Cointreau. In fact, it contained a bomb. But it did not explode, leaving von Schlabrendorff with a serious problem. He flew to Hitler's base, somehow retrieved the device, and on a train back to Berlin dismantled it and threw the pieces out of his carriage window. It was an amazing escape for both the Führer and for the army officer who had tried to assassinate the man he and many of his colleagues blamed for the Stalingrad disaster of 1942–43, when an entire army had been lost during a futile attempt to hold out on the Volga River.

Fast forward to the summer of 1944. In the west, Allied armies were threatening the Rhine; in the east, the Russians were preparing to drive through Poland towards Berlin. Disaffected German officers, together with civilians, were again looking at a way to bring the madness to an end. In fact, they had been plotting for more than two years. Their motives were manifold, ranging from opposing the Nazis' anti-semitism, trying to stop Hitler's increasingly erratic military policy that was leading Germany to catastrophe, to simply wanting to distance themselves from the war crimes that had been committed in their names since 1939.

Among them was a 36-year-old colonel on the staff of the Reserve Army. Claus von Stauffenberg, a member of a noble German family, had long been morally opposed to the Hitler regime. Badly wounded while serving in Tunisia, he had lost his left eye, his right hand, two fingers on his left hand and suffered severe leg wounds.

On 11 July 1944, von Stauffenberg was summoned to a conference at Berchtesgaden, the Alpine fortress that had become the Nazis' last stand,

Hitler's 'Eagle's Nest', a symbol of the madness of the Nazi regime, a place where so many decisions were made.

Von Stauffenberg arrived with a briefcase that contained a bomb, but the opportunity to use it did not present itself. Four days later, he took the device to Hitler's headquarters in East Prussia, the Wolfsschanze (Wolf's Lair). Again, the would-be assassin was thwarted. Hitler was called away on urgent business. On 20 July, von Stauffenberg tried again, when he was called to another meeting at the Wolf's Lair, a sealed and heavily guarded complex of bunkers, barracks, two airfields and a railway station set in a heavily wooded area near the small town of Ketrzyn.

It was a sweltering summer's day and Hitler moved the meeting from a concrete bunker, that was sealed with a heavy steel door, to a wooden barrack room. It was a decision that saved his life. Twenty-four men were standing or sitting around a substantial wooden table when von Stauffenberg arrived at 12.37pm. He saluted, apologised for being late for his presentation of new front-line divisions of the Reserve Army and placed his briefcase close to where Hitler stood poring over maps.

The bomb was primed to explode when acid from a glass globule that von Stauffenberg and his adjutant, Lieutenant Werner von Haeften, had prepared, bit into a wire spring. Von Stauffenberg excused himself to take a telephone call and left the room, but then another officer, finding the briefcase in his way, moved it further under the table. There was now a heavy wooden table leg between the bomb and Hitler. At 12.42pm, it exploded. Unlike the thick walls of a concrete bunker, the wooden hut provided little resistance. Its roof collapsed, windows were blown out, a hole was blasted in the floor where the bomb had been placed, there was a bluish-yellow flame and dark smoke enveloped those caught up in the blast.

One man, a stenographer, Heinrich Berger, was killed instantly when both his legs were blown off. Three others were mortally wounded, and the rest were all injured, some severely, others, remarkably, less so. There had been a second bomb, but von Stauffenberg had been unable to arm it in time. However, had he still placed it in his briefcase, then the detonation of the other would have still exploded it, doubling the effect. It was a stroke of great good fortune for the majority in the room.

Hitler was one of the fortunate ones. His right eardrum was perforated, he had burns to a leg, his trousers were in tatters and he was covered in dust. But he was still alive, and that afternoon he was able to show Benito Mussolini the site of the blast and give the Italian dictator a first-hand account.

In the meantime, chaos inevitably ensued. All communication was cut, and von Stauffenberg, who had seen the explosion from a distance, managed to return to the Bendlerblock, the Berlin headquarters of the Army Office and the Reserve Army, to help co-ordinate Operation Valkyrie – what would happen next, after Hitler had been killed. The plan had been thought out over many months: the Reserve Army would seize key installations, disarm the SS and arrest high-ranking Nazis. A provisional government would be formed with Carl Friedrich Goerdeler, a former mayor of Leipzig, as chancellor, and Ludwig Beck, a former chief of the German General Staff, as president. But, when no immediate word of Hitler's death was forthcoming, the plan stalled.

Then, a few hours later, news of the assassination attempt was broadcast by the German News Agency: 'Achtung! We are broadcasting an important announcement. Attempt to murder the Führer. The Führer is not hurt. A bomb attempt on the Führer's life was made today … The German people will learn with deep gratitude and satisfaction that the life of our Führer has not been harmed by this criminal attempt. Providence has protected the Führer from an attack made by an enemy who so often made use of murder, and who thought he could obtain by murder that which he could never attain through honest fighting.'

On 21 July, German Home Radio opened its first bulletin of the day with the words, 'The conspiracy against the Führer has completely collapsed.' The Nazi newspaper *Völkischer Beobachter* commented, 'The Berlin population, filled by its usual sense of duty, went to work calmly today. With his old steadfastness the Führer has immediately resumed his work. He knows that his soldiers will now fight as never before and will remain firm, becoming even more firm and more solid. The events of 20 July 1944 will imbue a new stream of energy into Germany. The small clique of generals who dared to betray their Führer and their people has perished by the intervention of justice and by their own miserable baseness … they have nothing in common with the German soldier who on all fronts is achieving miracles of faith and courage.' *Deutsche Allgemeine Zeitung* said that 'the German people will go back to work with relief that this attempted treason is finished and done with, and we may be certain that it will not be repeated'.

At one o'clock on the morning following the attack, Hitler had broadcast a message to the German people, telling them that he had appointed Heinrich Himmler as commander-in-chief of the Home Army, 'to create order once and for all'. He rambled on:

'For the third time an attempt on my life has been planned and carried out. If I speak to you today it is first in order you should hear my voice and that you should know that I myself am unhurt and well. Second, in order that you should know about a crime unparalleled in German history. A very small clique of ambitious, irresponsible and, at the same time, senseless and criminally stupid officers, have formed a plot to eliminate me and the German Wehrmacht command.

'The bomb exploded two metres to my right. One of those with me has died. I am myself completely unhurt. A number of collaborators very near to me were very severely injured. I myself sustained only some very minor scratches, bruises and burns. I regard this as confirmation of the task imposed on me by Providence to continue on the road of my life as I have done hitherto. For may I confess to the nation that since the days when I moved into the Wilhemstrasse, I had only one thought – to dedicate my life ever since I realised that the war could no longer be postponed.

'I have lived for worry, work, and worry only. Suddenly, at a moment when the German army are engaged in a bitter struggle, a small group emerged in Germany, just as in Italy, in the belief that they could repeat the 1918 stab in the back. But this time they have made a bad mistake. The circle of these conspirators is very small and there is no connection with the German Wehrmacht and, above all, none with the German people. It is a miniature group of criminal elements who will now be ruthlessly exterminated. I therefore now order that no military authority, no leader of any unit, no private in the field, is to obey any orders emanating from those groups of usurpers. I order that no civil authority is to accept orders from any official posts usurped by these usurpers. I also order that it is everyone's duty to arrest, or if they resist to kill at sight, anyone issuing or handing on such orders ... I am convinced that with the emergence of this quite tiny clique of traitors and destroyers there has, at long last, been created in our rear that atmosphere which the fighting front needs. For it is possible that out there, hundreds of thousands and millions of our brave men sacrificed their lives while at home a small, filthy, ambitious, self-seeking group should seem to sow the seeds of despair. This time we shall get quits with them in the way that National Socialists are accustomed. I am convinced that every decent officer, every gallant soldier, will comprehend this at this hour. What fate would have been in store for Germany had this attempt on my life succeeded is too horrible to think of. Every German, therefore, quite irrespective of who he may be, has the duty ruthlessly to call to book these elements at once, either to arrest them promptly or, if they should offer resistance of any kind, immediately to wipe them out. Orders have been issued to all troops. These will be blindly executed in accordance with the obedience characteristic of the Wehrmacht. It has again been granted to me that I should escape a fate which would have been terrible not just for me but for the German people. They see in this the pointing finger of Providence that I must and will carry on with my work'.

A reporter for the Bradford-based *Yorkshire Observer* who listened to the speech said, 'Hitler's voice sounded tired. His sentences were, at times, barely audible, and only once or twice did it recall the high pitch heard in other days. It was a fairly level almost conversational tone for the most part and it tailed off rather weakly.'

Britain's Home Secretary, Herbert Morrison, in a speech in London the following afternoon, said, 'There is something awkward there, and this sounds like the rather hysterical screeching of a man who feels that the foundations of his political power are shaking and being disturbed ... when I heard of the alleged attempt on his life, I wondered whether the story was a Goebbels fake for propaganda. I still cannot be sure. But I'm inclined to think that there is something shaky in the state of the German Reich.' Morrison warned against thinking that it meant 'the immediate or early termination of the war' but added, 'At any rate, we can say these events indicate stresses and strains within the military and possibly political structure of the German Reich.'

There was still confusion about what had actually happened. British United Press reported that 'the attempt on Hitler's life may have been made on his special train ... Such an attempt would be impossible to hide, thus forcing the Germans to issue a statement. Hitler may have been travelling through South Germany on his way to meet Mussolini.'

The *Liverpool Daily Post*'s London Letter column: 'Official circles here are not disposed to discuss the reported attempt on Hitler's life. A near miss from one of our bombs might very well cause the injuries, it was pointed out to me. A suggestion that an underground movement was now showing itself was not credited. We have a very shrewd idea of the trend of public opinion in Germany, expressed openly or not, and there is not the slightest encouragement for the idea that faith in Hitler is rapidly declining. Indeed, one who has had a close contact with Germany through well-informed sources, and who was a student of that country until the war, told me that German morale remained surprisingly high, and only imminent invasion on a vast scale would appear likely to break it down.'

On the other hand, the *Belfast Telegraph* rattled off a list of events that might suggest a German resistance movement was gaining momentum: 'It must have been cold comfort to the millions of Germans, depressed by the gloomy tidings from all their war fronts, to know that their carpet-chewing Führer had again cheated death. Only three months ago, rumours swept through neutral countries of an attempt on Hitler's life when his personal interpreter, Dr Schmidt, and other members of his entourage were injured in an air smash. There was never any confirmation from a German source of this alleged attempt, which took place when Hitler met Mussolini on 22–23 April. On 8 November 1939, a powerful time bomb exploded in the Burgerbrau beer cellar in Munich, a few minutes after Hitler had left the building. On that occasion Hitler had been addressing a meeting of members of the Nazi "Old Guard" in commemoration of the abortive Munich putsch of 1923. The bomb was secreted in an attic over the beer cellar. Hitler left the hall a few minutes ahead of schedule, owing to urgent business. In June 1938, when Hitler spoke in Vienna, three months after the Nazi seizure of Austria, a shot fired from a window killed a stormtrooper. A second attempt was made when he was crossing the Prater, a shot being fired at his car. In the same month Hitler's chauffer, Julius Schecks died mysteriously. It was widely surmised that he was killed during a bid to murder Hitler, and it was reported that he was shot in mistake for Hitler when they had changed seats at the wheel of Hitler's car. In 1935 reports of attacks on Hitler's life was so persistent that insurance premium rates against his death soared to the staggering figure of 60 per cent.

'After the famous "Night of the Long Knives" at the end of June 1934, when many highly placed Nazis, including Hitler's friend Röhm were murdered, Röhm's friends were reported to have formed an organisation called "The Avengers", which became more feared by Hitler than any other organisation in Germany.

'A significant feature about the latest attempt on Hitler's life is that no details as to the location have been allowed to leak out by the Nazi propaganda department, nor has any reason been given for the assembly of so many of his high-ranking collaborators.'

Reuters' 'continental observer' felt that the 'Nazi regime is in the throes of a life and death crisis'. 'There seems no doubt that the German army revolt is still on, and that a state of civil war exists in the Reich. Though the German News Agency claimed today that the conspiracy of dismissed army generals had collapsed, a speaker describing himself as an army officer broadcast on Frankfurt radio wavelength exhorting the army to resist "the Gestapo filth".'

The Frankfurt radio broadcast made by an unnamed German officer went out at 4.40am on 21 July. After a preliminary 'Achtung!' he said, 'We have our decorations for gallantry, but the only decoration we shall really merit is when we make good the crimes we have committed in Hitler's name. We have committed our crimes in fear of the Gestapo, and for this cowardice we can never forgive ourselves. We German officers await a wholehearted response. What will your response be? Some of you may declare that you never were a Nazi in your heart of hearts, or you were only a Nazi because you had to be, or you only pretended, or you stopped being a Nazi when things went bad at the front. Others will remain dumb. But such talk is not enough. Something more positive is demanded of you now, my comrades. Take the example of Lieutenant Herman Schneider, of the Waffen SS, whose division was stationed in Warsaw. Schneider was given orders to carry out a cruel punitive expedition against the Polish civilian population. He refused to stain the honour of the German officer corps. He resisted the orders of his superiors and came out in the open against our internal enemies. He lit a torch which must be carried forward by all German officers who prize their honour. What would your answer be my comrades? Your answer to your wives, your mothers, your children? Will you stand for the Gestapo filth? No! With your arms held openly in your hands, with a crystal clear awareness of what is at stake, close your ranks all of you. Let us not have just a single Herman Schneider, but a host of them, honourable German officers proceeding ...' At this point the broadcast abruptly ended.

At the news that Hitler had survived, events moved quickly in Germany. In order to cover up his own involvement, the commander of the Reserve Army, General Friedrich Fromm, gave up the conspirators. Von Stauffenberg, together with 55-year-old General Friedrich Olbricht, who had been helping to prepare Operation Valkyrie since 1942, and two others, von Haeften and Major Albrecht Metz von Quirnheim, was put to death by firing squad in the inner courtyard of the Bendlerblock on 21 July. Eventually, around 200 people thought to be involved in the plot to kill Hitler were executed. Von Stauffenberg's older brother, Berthold, was one of eight men slowly strangled with piano wire at Plötzensee prison in Berlin, the whole scene filmed for Hitler's later viewing pleasure.

Chapter 4

The Liberation of Paris

The pulse of Paris is throbbing back to life again after the most amazing twenty-four hours in its stirring history.

Noel Monks, Sunday Dispatch

'I do not believe there has been another day like this in history. I am in Paris – free Paris, surrounded by a million people who are mad with joy. … My eyes are wet with tears. And every man in the American army with me is crying too. If you knew these Parisians and knew what they have suffered … you would understand how and why they mob us and kiss us. How they just stand and cheer themselves hoarse, while in between times they wipe the tears from their own faces … Bigger and bigger grew the crowds as we drove. They were pelting us with flowers, paper balls, with flags and everything that would show their joy … I can still hardly believe that Paris is free. I do not think that Paris believes it either.'

Thus, on Saturday, 26 August 1944, four years after the city had fallen to the Nazis, an unnamed *Sunday Pictorial* war correspondent described his arrival in the French capital. In front of him he saw two French soldiers standing on a tank, performing 'cricket-field miracles' as they caught every tomato thrown their way, and then ate the lot. Women and girls stood on abandoned German 88cm guns to gain better vantage points. There were thousands in the streets, all smartly dressed. It seemed as if everyone had rushed home to put on their Sunday best before rushing back into the city centre to spend the rest of the day, and most of the night, in revelry.

Paris had fallen on 14 June 1940, one month after the Wehrmacht invaded France. It was decided not to defend the capital. Eight days later, France signed an armistice, and a puppet French state was created with its headquarters at the spa town of Vichy in central France, and with First World War hero Marshal Philippe Pétain as the prime minister of a collaborationist fascist regime.

Enter French army officer Charles de Gaulle, who on 5 June had been appointed minister of war by Prime Minister Paul Reynaud. As the new regime was formed, de Gaulle left for England, where Winston Churchill recognised him as the leader of the 'Free French'. And, despite being excluded from the planning for Operation Overlord, when the US Army entered Paris on 25 August 1944, de Gaulle and his 2nd Armoured Division, veterans of the North African campaign, were there too. Later that day, de Gaulle announced that the French Forces of the Interior (FFI), his formal name for the Resistance movement – small cells of armed men known in more rural areas as the Maquis – would be integrated into the French Army, while the Milice, the Vichy paramilitary militia created in January 1943, would be dissolved. His attempt to incorporate the FFI into the regular army was not met with universal approval, however. In Paris, many of the Resistance movement believed that they had done their duty in helping to liberate the capital. They were not now keen to go on foreign service. In September, the *Aberdeen Press and Journal* reported, 'They are ready to remain on garrison duty but are handicapped by the poverty of their establishment and equipment. Bands of young men, some of them mere boys, driving or marching about Paris armed with revolvers and rifles are not always viewed with favour by civilians. Their enthusiasm for the work of purgation [of collaborators] has led them to make numerous arrests without authority.'

Before D-Day, de Gaulle had worked hard to unify the various arms of the Resistance that were sabotaging power lines, communication networks, fuel storage depots, bridges, railway lines and roads that served the needs of both Vichy France and the Nazi occupiers.

By 1944, in Paris no German soldier could feel safe walking alone. The official Nazi line was that all Resistance fighters were either Communists (and many were) or Jews – probably both – and that 90 per cent of them were of foreign origin. To underline the point, when, in February, twenty-three of twenty-four 'résistants' put on trial in Paris were executed, posters carrying photographs of ten of them were plastered around the capital. Five were Polish, two were Hungarian Jews, one was Spanish, one was an Italian Communist and their leader was an Armenian. 'Are these the liberators?' asked the posters.

On 28 June, Philippe Henriot, the Vichy Government's Propaganda Secretary, was shot, in front of his wife, at his official residence in Paris, by Resistance fighters disguised as members of the Milice. Joseph Darnard, the head of the Milice and now Vichy's Secretary of State for the Maintenance of Order, had already appealed for volunteers to join the fight against the Resistance. 'The orders are clear,' he said. 'Consider as enemies of France … the members of the alleged secret army … Fight against saboteurs … track down all who seek to undermine the morale of our units … I now mobilise the reserves of the Milice … for the revival of a France proud and free.' It was time for the hardest of crackdowns.

More than at any time since 1940, the 'open city' of Paris was now looking like a city at war. Allied air raids were aimed at the industrial belt that surrounded the capital, and columns of military trucks took German troops towards the Normandy front, while ambulances brought wounded soldiers in the opposite direction, away from the fighting. Everyone realised that eventually the incoming traffic would be comprised not of exhausted Germans but of Allied forces. Liberation was surely on its way. But when? Allied eyes were fixed on the German border. Eisenhower did not want to divert valuable assets away from the advance eastwards. Paris, no longer a military objective, could be besieged and then liberated when it was more convenient. De Gaulle, however, urged that the city should be taken back as soon as possible. While many members of the Resistance were loyal to de Gaulle, the Communists commanded power and influence. If they succeeded in liberating Paris before the Allies, then the re-establishment of a democratic government would be threatened.

On 13 August, word spread that the Germans were beginning to disarm the 20,000-strong Paris police, the overwhelming majority of whom were sympathetic to the Resistance and provided the largest source of armaments to it. The police went on strike, discarding their uniforms but retaining their weapons to join the Resistance on the city's streets. A formal declaration was issued by the FFI: 'The hour of liberation has come … Today it is the duty of the whole body of the police to join the FFI … You will aid the FFI in putting down anyone who continues to serve the enemy in anyway … Police who do not obey these orders will be considered traitors and collaborators … March with the people of Paris to the final battle.'

The new German military commander of Paris, 49-year-old General Dietrich von Choltitz, had been in the post for only one week. He now faced general insurrection. He also found himself in charge of mostly demoralised conscripts. Many public buildings fell to the Resistance, roads were barricaded, and German vehicles and communications sabotaged. A ceasefire brokered by the Swedish consul-general in Paris, Raoul Nordling, was ignored and sporadic fighting continued.

On 20 August, Paris Radio broke four days of silence. An unfamiliar voice said,

'This is Paris. This is Paris. Important announcement. Irresponsible elements in Paris have taken up arms against the occupation authorities. This revolt will be vigorously suppressed and, if necessary, without consideration. I make one more appeal to the population to keep their heads. Only a reasonable attitude will make it possible to avoid bloodshed among the innocent and to save the city from damage.'

The proclamation fixed a curfew from 9pm to 7am, forbade access to highways 'in districts which might become military zones' and ordered that all theatres, cinemas and cafes close. The population were to keep all windows shut, to leave front doors ajar during the night, gatherings of more than three people were banned and anyone giving information to the enemy would be shot as a spy. The proclamation was repeated over Paris Radio three times. The German Overseas News Agency quoted a Berlin Foreign Office spokesman:

'Paris will be spared military operations just as we spared it in 1940. The fate of the city is in the hands of its inhabitants. If they want martial law they can have it. It is up to them [the Maquis].'

The situation, though, was out of control and, on 23 August, Hitler ordered that Paris must not fall into enemy hands 'except as a field of ruins'. Explosives began to be laid under Paris's many landmarks and bridges, but the order was not carried out. Von Choltitz later took credit for that, giving rise to his being known as the 'Saviour of Paris'. It was later claimed that General Hans Speidel had also played a major role in thwarting Hitler's plans to demolish Paris. In fact, von Choltitz, wishing to deflect blame, had telephoned Speidel and asked for further instructions on how to carry out Hitler's orders. Speidel said that no such order had been passed through him. He realised that von Choltitz was looking for someone to share the blame. They both now considered that Hitler was insane. There was a hidden mutual understanding of what had to be done – nothing. Both men also feared that their conversation was being overheard by the Gestapo. Speidel was also under suspicion and, a few weeks later, was arrested and accused of being involved in the July 1944 plot to assassinate Hitler. He was held prisoner for seven months before escaping into Allied custody.

The events of those few days in August convinced Eisenhower that de Gaulle was right – Paris must be taken now. The task was given to General Omar Bradley, who told General Jacque Leclerc, commander of the French 2nd Armoured Division, to contact the German garrison in the city. He would be supported by the US 4th Infantry Division. On 23 August, the French advanced on Paris from the north and the Americans from the south.

On 24 August, the 2nd Armoured Division crossed the Seine and reached the suburbs of Paris, to be met by an ecstatic civilian population. Just before midnight, French troops reached the Hôtel de Ville in the very heart of Paris.

Bradley had expected them earlier, and, growing impatient at what he saw as an avoidable delay as the French enjoyed being greeted in every village en route with flowers and kisses, had already ordered his men into the city, commenting that he 'couldn't wait for them to dance their way into Paris'.

During the night, most of the German garrison had fled or surrendered. Those who chose to fight on were soon overcome. On the morning of 25 August, French troops swept clear the western half of Paris while the Americans cleared the eastern part. The new Free French radio station reported that von Choltitz had signed a surrender at Montparnasse railway station, in front of General Leclerc and 'Colonel Rol' (Henri Tanguy, the commander of the FFI).

On 26 August, the *Aberdeen Press and Journal* reported that General de Gaulle, as head of the Provisional French Government, had entered Paris at 7pm the previous day: 'A Paris radio broadcast announced earlier that the German commander in the French capital had surrendered to General Leclerc, hero of Chad and commander of the 2nd French Armoured Division, which entered the city on Thursday night to complete its liberation. Orders were given to subordinate Nazi commanders to cease fire and hoist the white flag. Weapons were to be collected and surrendered intact and the Germans were to gather without weapons at specified points. On his entry into the capital General de Gaulle was received by the prefecture of police, and at the Hôtel de Ville by the new prefect. In a short speech he said. "I wish simply and from the bottom of my heart to say to you, Vive Paris."'

British newspapers continued to paint vivid pictures of the scene. Noel Monks of the *Sunday Dispatch*: '... Parisians awoke yesterday a free people again, and thousands thronged the streets soon after dawn, eager to assure themselves that they had not been dreaming. What happened in this city between dawn and dusk on Friday is too fantastic even for a dream, but the stark reality is that Paris found its soul and its freedom and is back again in the life of the democratic world. Parisians took their just revenge, not in violence but with that derision and contempt for which they are famous. The jackbooted "supermen" who came goose-stepping into the city four years ago were herded through the streets an unkempt, terrified, broken rabble with their hands high in the air and their faces twitching with fear, treading on each other's heels in their frenzy to obey their captors orders of "Vite! Vite!" I saw one lot of Germans brought up from the sewers where they had been hiding from the Maquis, emerge on to the Champs Elysees. Their uniforms were caked with filth, and mud squelched from their boots.

'... From the windows of the Ritz Hotel, 250 Germans, most of them young officers, had been shooting across the Place de la Concorde since dawn. As I arrived on the scene, the hotel was rushed by 100 Maquis while several tanks engaged six Tiger tanks parked near the Champs Elysees. The Germans quit cold. They had no heart for hand-to-hand combat, so they waved white towels from the luxurious bathrooms and came trooping down the thickly carpeted staircase. I sneaked into the foyer and watched the Germans surrender to a woman, the wife of a young Maquis leader.

'... The barricades are now coming down in Paris, but the excitement is not yet over for Parisians. Shops and restaurants have not yet opened but the civil authorities have plans in hand for liberation celebrations on a grand scale – and who knows how to celebrate better than Parisians?'

In *The Sunday Sun*, distinguished writer Leonard Mosley said, 'Paris awoke this morning with sore heads but happy hearts, and so, in fact, did we all. For Paris yesterday gave all those of us who entered with the liberating army a welcome with flowers and embraces, tears and champagne, such as only this great capital can give – and gave us that welcome while battles still raged in the Place de la Republique, the Tuilleries Gardens, and all around the Champs Elysees. Now once more this afternoon Paris is celebrating again. Many Nazis have surrendered, and many swastika flags have been hauled down, and many snipers hunted from the rooftops ... the last one was killed at 5:30am.'

A man asked Mosley whether it was true what the Germans said – that the Allies had bombed French industry because they intended to profit by it after the war. Mosley told him that the Allies' only desire was to set France up again as a strong European power.

'Well, you see,' said the man, 'we in the French factories have continuously sabotaged the German efforts to make us turn out war materials. Every time we had the chance we did something to make the article useless. We did not work hard either and production fell by 70 per cent in spite of all the Germans could do. Then you bombed us, and the Germans told me that you wanted our industries. I'm enormously relieved to know the story is false.'

Mosley wrote,

'Finally let me say that the Parisians hate the Germans with the Gallic fervour. They could not counterfeit their emotions or the manner in which their faces screwed up in hate when they spoke of the Nazis. Perhaps their greatest moment was when French tanks rolled into Paris.

They had expected the Americans, and, when their own men came, they became hysterical with joy.'

The *Sunday Post* reported,

'Although the city is desperately short of things to eat and drink there is no shortage of lipstick. As we drove in, my face became covered in a violent rash from the kisses I received from hundreds of excited mademoiselles.'

A shortage of food was certainly a major problem. Amidst all the joyous scenes, a group of women gazed at an army truck going by, full of food. They looked sad. People were now beginning to remember how weary and how hungry Paris was. Throughout the occupation they had been feeding relatively well, but for the past seven days few people had seen any bread or milk. The *Sunday Pictorial* correspondent again:

'There is certainly need for food here today. I am told that the most famous restaurant in the world – the Café de la Paix – is open again tonight. But it is selling only apple juice. And I cannot see how, in the middle of this fighting, we can hope to spare the transport for thousands of tons of food that will be needed. But we are trying. Tonight I hear that 3,000 tons [2,721 tonnes] of food have already arrived for hungry Parisians.'

Plans for supplying emergency food and medical stores to the people of Paris had been drawn up by the Allied Army's Civil Aviation Affairs Division, it was announced later that day by the Supreme Headquarters Allied Expeditionary Force (SHAEF). First supplies would be sent into Paris as soon as the military situation permitted. The most difficult problem was one of transport. Indispensable foodstuffs and medical supplies would reach the citizens of Paris when some of the lorries and trucks now in use on the battlefronts could be spared. In preparation for this, the French were recruiting many hundreds of drivers to collect and load the supplies and take them to Paris. Distribution of food within the city would be the responsibility of the French authorities, but Allied civil affairs officers on General Eisenhower's staff would assist their French colleagues during the early stages of the distribution programme.

The *Daily Herald* had suggested that, when the liberation of Paris was announced, it should be welcomed in Britain by the ringing of church bells. 'For this event signals something more even than a tremendous military victory. Paris is a symbol to all men of the cause of liberty, equality and fraternity. So let us ring our bells. Let us broadcast their clamour to France as a token of our rejoicing at our great neighbours' triumphant emergence from four years' trial during which her people have borne themselves with glorious courage. Let us broadcast peals to the world so that they may be heard in the countries which are still under the rule of gauleiter and Gestapo, and so that also they may sound a knell in the ears of the Nazi tyrants.'

The People's 'Let's Talk It Over' column summed it up well:

'In the Tube lift an errand boy was whistling *La Marseillaise*. He was a tousle-headed urchin of fourteen who would have been far better at school. The chances are he picked up the tune in Soho the night before. But there was a Frenchman standing beside me, a lean, bronzed, middle-aged man in uniform with a row of ribbons on his chest, who look kindly upon this lad. And almost under his breath I heard him take up one line of his country's immortal anthem: "Le jour de gloire est arrivé!" Truly for France, and for all men who love freedom more than life, the day of glory has arrived. Paris has won back its independence and a keen wind is tearing gaps in the pall of darkness which has overhauled the continent for four years … The soul of Paris has never changed. It was almost suffocated, but now it can breathe again.'

Things were definitely beginning to return to normal in the French capital. On 14 September 1945, the *Gloucestershire Echo* reported

'Frenchwomen will get "smokes" on ration': 'French women, who until now were not entitled to cigarettes, which are rationed in France, will be allowed forty a month at the end of the year, the Ministry of Finance announces … The monthly ration for men will be increased next month, from 120 to 140, because of improved supplies of tobacco.'

Along with the rest of France, Paris could indeed breathe again – even through cigarette smoke.

Chapter 5

One Bridge Too Far

We knew from experience that the only way to draw the tooth of an airborne landing with an inferior force is to drive right into it.

SS Major Josef 'Sepp' Krafft

On Sunday, 18 September 1944, a member of General Eisenhower's staff broadcast a statement calling on the people of the Netherlands for one last supreme effort:

'The hour for which you have been waiting so long has struck. Now that Allied forces are on your soil and the Netherlands forces are acting with them, your full assistance and obedience to the orders of the Supreme Commander are essential for the early liberation of the Netherlands.'

Dutch Resistance forces were told, 'Conduct operations against the enemy according to the rules of war. In the event of any atrocities by the German forces, collect all evidence. Follow precisely the orders from HRH Prince Bernhard. Do not indulge in any organised outbursts of violence ... Do not attempt any mass rising in still unliberated areas ... This is a supreme moment. Fulfil your task loyally. If all play their part the liberation of the Netherlands will be achieved soon. Long live the Netherlands.'

After D-Day, the Allies had made rapid progress across France against disorganised and increasingly demoralised German forces. However, following the liberation of Paris in late August, the Allies regrouped and resupplied, as a result of which their advance slowed. Some American commanders wanted to go it alone, but Eisenhower insisted that the advance on the Rhine should continue to include the British, with Montgomery's 21st Army Group pushing on in the north of a broad front with the Americans in the centre and the south of the thrust. In early September, the British 2nd Army, commanded by Lieutenant General Sir Miles Dempsey, liberated Brussels and Antwerp, although the latter's port could not be used until it had been cleared of the remaining German defenders. The allocation of resources to Operation Market Garden meant that it would be October before – thanks to heroic fighting by the 1st Canadian Amy with units from other nations – Allied shipping could use the Scheldt Estuary.

That summer, the Allies had come up with an ambitious plan – codenamed 'Market Garden' – to cross the Rhine, advance into northern Germany and, if that did not mean that the war might be over before Christmas, at least vital progress could be made before winter set in.

The operation's success rested on the seizing of three key river bridges in the Netherlands – at Eindhoven, Nijmegen and, furthest from the start line, at Arnhem, as well as two smaller bridges between Eindhoven and Nijmegen, at Veghel and Grave. The attack would be carried out by the 101st and 82nd US Airborne Divisions, and the British 1st Airborne Division, with the Polish 1st Parachute Brigade temporarily attached.

Once all the bridges had been secured then the British 30 Corps would cross the Rhine and its tributaries, and outflank the Siegfried Line, the German defensive line that began on the border with the Netherlands and continued for more than 390 miles (627km) to the Swiss border. Then it would press onwards into the Ruhr, the beating heart of German industry.

The airborne divisions landed on 17 September. It was one of the largest airborne operations in history. From 'somewhere in Holland', Combined Press correspondent Alan Wood was among several journalists who painted the scene for British newspaper readers:

'The field is now littered with gliders like broken toys. Then come the parachutists, dropping in the nearby field – hundreds of them. I mean literally hundreds of them, filling the sky simultaneously, spilling out of Dakotas flying very low, the parachutes filling out like many coloured flowers, prostrate in the sky, some blue, some red, some yellow. It seemed that nearly all dropped down safely … Once something dropped dead, straight from a plane to the ground at our feet, and we all had a moment of sickening horror. Then we realised that it was only a kit bag of equipment, and we all picked ourselves up.'

Just in case German troops did not appreciate the full measure of what was happening, over Moscow radio Major General Arno von Lenski, former commander of the 24th German Panzer Division who had been captured by the Soviets at Stalingrad, broadcast to his former colleagues in the Wehrmacht: 'An unprecedented air offensive will be launched against German cities. The squeeze is on and with a sure hand Allied generals are compressing the fronts. I can tell you that every village, every little hamlet will be involved during the next few weeks as there is no power on earth that can stop the Allies now. These last weeks of war will bring about bloodshed on your side such has never yet has been witnessed in history.' After the war, von Lenski would be formally acknowledged as 'a victim of fascism' and serve as a politician in the newly created German Democratic Republic. For now, though, he sat in Moscow as the battle for Arnhem, the 'bridge too far', unfolded.

The Americans had been successful in securing the bridges at Eindhoven and Nijmegen, while the British were tasked with seizing the road bridge over the Neder Rijn, the Lower Rhine, at Arnhem. Almost, 10,000 men from the 1st Airborne Division, under the command of 43-year-old Major General Roy Urquhart, and the 1st Polish Independent Parachute Brigade, were dropped, but they landed 7 miles (11km) from the bridge. The hastily planned Operation Market Garden had suffered many problems. A shortage of transport aircraft had meant that airborne troops were dropped in three separate lifts, while thick fog over England and low cloud over the target areas had hampered sending in further troops and supplies. It also meant that, because the landing zones had to be protected, it left only three battalions of the Parachute Brigade to push on to the bridge at Arnhem. Only one, relatively lightly armed, battalion – many weapons had been modified to fit into gliders – reached its objective. The others were trapped in a pocket at the village of Oosterbeek 2.5 miles (4.2km) to the west, where they held on for nine days before being ordered to withdraw.

It was the 2nd Parachute Battalion, commanded by Lieutenant Colonel John Frost, together with Royal Engineers and a Recce Company, that reached the bridge at 8pm and secured the northern end. In the face of repeated German attacks, they managed to hold it for more than three days, twenty-four hours longer than they had been ordered to do so until relieved by ground forces.

They were not equipped to defend themselves against two SS Panzer divisions that Allied intelligence had failed to detect until the last minute, and the reinforcements could not reach them in time. Traffic jams on a narrow causeway, German counterattacks and destroyed bridges all combined to delay the progress of the British 30th Corps, that had helped the US 82nd Airborne Division capture the bridge at Nijmegen. On 25 September, the British and Poles were ordered to withdraw from the ever-decreasing Arnhem bridgehead. Only about 2,500 troops from the 1st Airborne Division could be brought back across the Rhine to 30th Corps' position. Frost himself had been wounded by shrapnel and, during a short truce, he and other casualties were evacuated and became prisoners of war along with hundreds of others. Almost 1,500 had been killed and more than 6,500 taken prisoner, many of them badly wounded. The heroics of those that reached Arnhem was reflected in the award of five Victoria Crosses.

It was the Dutch civilians who suffered most. More than 3,500 were killed, almost 20,000 badly injured and more than 200,000 made homeless as punishment for aiding the Allies. Eighteen thousand men, women and children in the northern Netherlands died from starvation in what became known as the Hunger Winter. The bridge at Arnhem had been the key to the whole operation and it would be another four months before the Allies crossed the Rhine again and finally captured Germany's industrial heartland. The city of Arnhem itself was not liberated until April 1945.

In the days after troops had been evacuated from Arnhem, accounts of heroism began to appear in British newspapers. A *News Chronicle* reporter told how he had spent the day with a thirty-strong group of civilian pilots in unprotected Anson aircraft, who had taken vital supplies to the men at Arnhem:

'With only compass and map, they delivered medical supplies, blood plasma, mortar-bombs, small arms and petrol in weather which only men of their highly selected and specially trained type could fly through alone. Sometimes each man made two journeys a day. Since Monday they have taken more than 152 plane loads and brought back Arnhem wounded and pilots who bailed out into the Rhine. But they did not have a single casualty. "As long as birds can fly we will," said First Officer Edward Pyatt of Wolverhampton. I watched him peel off his Mae West and jacket to squeeze in head-first through the window of his plane which was too full of supplies for him to get in by the door. Captain L. Thornhill of Potters Head, Somerset, at 6ft 5ins the tallest pilot in Air Transport Auxiliary which has 700 members, brought back yesterday six English and American airmen who had bailed out into the Rhine. "They had been hiding in woods for seven weeks," he said. "They wore ragged slacks and jerseys and somehow hiked back to Brussels."'

Air Commodore Gerard d'Erlanger told how, at 4pm on the day of the Arnhem landings, he had been asked to put together the service, which was called Air Movements Flight. At dawn the following day, 20 Anson were ready. They had been gathered from all over the country, serviced, their seats removed, and bodies painted black and white.

'Many of the pilots had never flown over the Continent before,' he said. 'They were shown, on a map, a corridor to guide them, and their only instructions were to keep to it. They get no help from the ground, and sometimes they have to dip around among the rhubarb fields to find roads and railway cuttings to follow. Over the Channel they trusted their dinghies – and hope. Lawyers are busy trying to work out what would happen to them if they fell into enemy hands. They class as civilians.'

Montgomery sent a message to Urquhart: 'There is no shadow of doubt that, had you failed, operations elsewhere would have been gravely compromised. You did not fail, and all is well elsewhere. I would like all Britain to know that in your final message from the Arnhem area you said, "All will be ordered to breakout rather than surrender. We have attempted our best and we will continue to do our best as long as possible." And all Britain will say to you, "You did your best. And all did your duty. And we are proud of you." In the annals of the British Army there are many glorious deeds, but there can be few episodes more glorious than the epic of Arnhem. In years to come it will be a great thing for a man to be able to say, "I fought at Arnhem." Please give my best wishes and my grateful thanks to every officer and man in your division.'

'Dunkirk was a quiet weekend' compared to the fighting at Arnhem, according to one of the airborne troops interviewed by a Reuters correspondent in Brussels on 29 September. One graphic story was told by Lieutenant John McCartney of Edinburgh whose men held the final sector that became known as 'Hellfire Corner'. After landing, he advanced with a machine-gun section to take a village, and the men dug in between the Amin road and the riverbank. After German shells had blown up four or five of their ammunition trucks, they were cornered. They suffered heavy casualties and eventually withdrew to the west of Arnhem.

McCartney, who commanded No. 28 Medium Machine Gun Platoon, 1st Border, said, 'The enemy came up in strength from the west, and heavy mortaring started. But we replied and inflicted severe casualties. I took our machine-gun section to the forward company of the forward brigade, and we dug in in positions at a road junction which eventually became known as Hellfire Corner – and God knows it was too. We stayed there from Wednesday until Monday, with our casualties mounting steadily. Twenty-two attacks by infantry were made during that time, all of which were beaten off with heavy casualties to the enemy.

'On Sunday we were mortared relentlessly from dawn to dusk. We had orders to hold our positions, but we were without food and ammunition because a lot of resupplies which got through was, by this time, within the enemy lines. We had promises of relief for three days, but they were not forthcoming. On Sunday, we also had attacks by tanks with flamethrowers and self-propelled guns. By that time most of our anti-tank guns had been wiped out, but our machine-guns were still in action, and we held on to our corner.

'On Monday we had orders to withdraw to the river. At eight o'clock that evening there was heavy shelling from our guns from the south bank of the river on the enemy positions on our front. The German reply was to open up with everything he had on us. For two and a half hours we had the worst shelling of the whole nine days.

'At 10.50 on Monday night I withdrew my machine-gun and anti-tank sections. It was a dark night, windy and raining, and the noise was simply dreadful. It was a nightmare journey to the beach. We passed a gasometer blown up with dozens of bodies around and machine-guns firing everywhere. When we reached the riverbank, all we could see was a couple of old rowing boats riddled with machine gun bullets, and the bodies of English soldiers inside. After reconnaissance we made contact with light motor boats and were ferried across.'

For his actions at Arnhem, Lieutenant McCartney was recommended for the Military Cross by Major Stuart Cousens, acting commander of the battalion. Part of his citation reads:

'Lieutenant McCartney was tireless in his efforts to kill the enemy, personally directing the fire of his guns; he moved from one gun position to another, completely regardless of the danger from mortar and shells, to encourage his men to greater efforts. He personally assisted in bringing up more ammunition under continuous heavy fire, and when it became necessary he took over personal control of one of the guns. His tireless energy, devotion to duty, and disregard of danger were an inspiration to all ranks, and his efforts were largely responsible for the attack being repelled with considerable loss to the enemy.' Although the recommendation was passed at brigade level, it was ultimately refused.

The *Rochdale Observer* summed it all up:

'History alone can decide whether the risk of landing these men so far ahead of General Dempsey's armour and infantry was a legitimate one to take, and also whether the gains of the operation have justified the losses ... At least we can salute with reverent pride the superb heroism which made the airborne troops' stand at Arnhem one of the most glorious pages in military history. The episode will also have an astringent effect on the rather sloppy overconfidence which our successes have inspired in some quarters. It makes us realise that victory may still be a long way off and that the fiercest fighting of the war is probably yet to come.'

Chapter 6

Freckleton – a Grim Reminder

The village of Freckleton suffers as many European villages have suffered and the more keenly because her tragedy was so unexpected. That is war.

Manchester Evening News

On the morning of Wednesday, 23 August 1944, the villagers of Freckleton on the Fylde coast went about their business as usual. The war news was encouraging. German forces were being pushed back eastwards and, although the situation in Paris was confusing, it seemed that the French capital might be on the verge of being liberated. And as it attempted to enter the English Channel, a U-boat was sunk in daylight when a B-24 Liberator of RAF Coastal Command finished it off with depth charges as the Mosquito pilots who had earlier raked it with cannon shells looked on.

That same morning, at Warton aerodrome, just over a mile from Freckleton, two refurbished Liberators took off on routine test flights. They were flown by experienced US Air Force pilots First Lieutenant John Allen Lucas Bloemendal and First Lieutenant Peter Manassero. The RAF had handed over Warton to the Americans in 1942. The following year it was reopened as the USAF's Base Air Depot No. 2 (BAD-2), staffed by 5,000 US personnel. Every type of American aircraft used in the European theatre of operations visited BAD-2, and tens of thousands of aero-engines, armaments, radios, instruments parachutes and accessories would be processed there.

On that August morning in 1944, both Liberators headed out over the Lancashire countryside, but after only a few minutes Bloemendal drew Manassero's attention to an odd-looking cloud formation to the south-east. At about the same time, a weather station reported a violent storm approaching Warton. Both aircraft were ordered back to their base. By the time they arrived over the airfield, it was raining so heavily that it was impossible for those on the ground to see across the road. There was thunder and lightning, and a local meteorological station reported winds of almost 60mph (96.5kph). At Warton, the cloud cover was so low and so thick that, although it was a summer's morning, it seemed more like night.

Warton sent out a general call to all aircraft to go north of the storm and await recall when it had passed. Manassero acknowledged the call, but there was no word from Bloemendal. The two bombers had already each lowered their landing gear and, flying 100yd apart, were lining up for a runway. Manassero retracted his landing gear and climbed away. For Bloemendal in 'Classy Chassis II', it was too late. Already close to the ground and with wings almost vertical, the B-24's right wingtip caught a tree and was ripped away as it hit a building. The wing ploughed into the ground and through a hedge. The fuselage partly demolished three houses as well as hitting the Sad Sack snack bar that was a favourite with American airmen based at Warton. Further, and unimaginable, tragedy was to follow. The fuselage carried on across Lytham Road. Part of it struck the infants' wing of Freckleton Holy Trinity School, and fuel from ruptured tanks ignited. There was no chance for anyone to survive the sea of flames. Efforts by BAD-2's fire service who, together with other servicemen and villagers, battled for twenty minutes before the first National Fire Service appliances arrived, were courageous but futile.

The death toll was sixty-one: Bloemendal and his fellow crewmen, Technical Sergeant James Parr, the co-pilot and Sergeant Gordon Kinney, the flight engineer; four RAF personnel, seven USAF personnel and seven civilians were killed in the Sad Sack snack bar; and two teachers and thirty-eight children aged between 4 and 6 perished at the school. It was the biggest loss of life in a single aviation accident in Britain during the Second World War. The teachers killed were 64-year-old Louisa Lee Hulme, who came from Manchester, and 20-year-old Jennie Hall, who was in only her second day of employment at the school where she had been a pupil. Both died in hospital, Jennie Hall the day after the crash, Louisa Hulme the day after that. One teacher, Doris Gardener, was visiting her sick mother, and so her life was spared. She lived to the age of ninety-one before dying in 2010.

The official report into the crash records that the exact cause was unknown, although investigators concluded that Lieutenant Bloemendal had not realised the danger until he made his approach to land. By then, given the violent conditions, he had insufficient altitude and speed to manoeuvre. Structural failure may also have occurred, although the aircraft was completely destroyed, rendering impossible any investigation into that likelihood. It was recommended that, before they were posted to Britain, pilots trained in the United States should be warned about the dangers of British thunderstorms, which could occasionally be every bit as perilous as those often encountered in the southern United States.

The funerals of the victims of the Freckleton air disaster were held only three days later. The service took place in Freckleton on 26 August. The majority of the child victims together with teacher Jennie Hall and a number of civilians killed in the Sad Sack snack bar were buried in a communal grave in the village's Holy Trinity Churchyard. It had been dug in the shade of a row of slender poplars by American soldiers. At Preston, from where special buses were run to carry former Freckleton residents returning to the village for the funerals, holidaymakers bound for Blackpool stood back in respectful silence to let them past. Many mourners carried wreaths, and bus drivers and conductors helped them stack their floral tributes before boarding. On every bus there were also American servicemen also making the sad seven-and-a-half-mile journey.

In Freckleton itself, the blinds were drawn down at every house and the streets of the village were lined with mourners, often standing six deep, as the procession passed. Crowds stood around the parish church next to the partly demolished schoolroom. The entire churchyard at the front was carpeted with wreaths. More were constantly being unloaded. Among them were many small bunches of flowers addressed in childish handwriting to dead schoolmates. An enormous anchor of white chrysanthemums with the letters 'ARP' in yellow flowers came from the chief warden, deputy chief and all members of the Kirkham and Fylde Wardens Service.

There was a bunch of six lilies, which had been addressed care of Freckleton's postmaster, in memory of three evacuee children who lost their lives. It was sent by a school friend named Clive from North Cheam in Surrey. On each of the small coffins, made by the Americans, in classrooms which were still standing in the school lay posies of cottage flowers.

The service was limited to members of the bereaved families. Each family had five tickets for the church, which held only 200 people. The children whose coffins were carried by American soldiers were buried first, in the communal grave at the end of the churchyard. The adults were buried afterwards. The three airmen from the Liberator were buried in a US cemetery in the south of England before being later returned to their home states. Bloemendal was finally laid to rest in Ramsey County, Minnesota; Parr in Duval County, Florida: Kinney in Tillman County, Oklahoma.

The Bishop of Blackburn, Dr Wilfred Askwith, told the mourners, 'I don't want you to say that this tragedy was the will of God. Tragedies of this kind that happen in this world are not due to the will of God but to the fact that men who have been given free wills have done what they have done for the good world which God created.'

The *Manchester Evening News* commented:

'Lancashire has for long escaped the sudden agonising tragedies of war, but one came upon us yesterday afternoon when the small children of the village of Freckleton were almost wiped out by the crash of a blazing Liberator. It was a grim reminder that so long as war lasts, no part of the country can be safe from the swift blaze of death. The evil thing is no respect of age, and it knows no boundaries. Every day thousands of bombers fill the skies over our English countryside, moving securely over children at play and old people at their chimney corners. Great attention is paid to safety and considering their numbers and the kind of work they have to do, accidents are astonishingly few. But a fatal chance overtook that Liberator as it passed across Lancashire, and a fatal chance brought it down on an infants' school …'

Freckleton was by no means the only British community visited by such horror during the Second World War. Only two days after the funerals, a USAAF Douglas DC-4 from Boston, Massachusetts, via Gander and Keflavik, crashed into houses near Prestwick, the Scottish airport that was one the world's busiest air hubs with thousands of American and Canadian aircraft flying in and out.

Coming in at 12.40am that day, during poor visibility, the DC-4 hit several homes. The dead numbered twenty-five: six crew; fourteen passengers; and five on the ground – four war workers who were killed together with 6-year-old Irene Haswell, the granddaughter of the men's landlady. The little girl died on the way to hospital.

Jean M'Gregor, who lived almost opposite the scene, told the *Aberdeen Evening Express*, 'I was in bed when I heard a plane coming low over the house. Almost immediately there was a crash. I rushed to the window, threw up the blind and looked out. So fierce was the glow of fire opposite the house that my eyes were blinded …'

Mr J. Anderson, whose house was also gutted, told of a miraculous escape for his family. Mr Anderson, his wife, his 74-year-old mother-in-law, his two sons and an airman from Nova Scotia who was staying with them, all survived. He found his mother-in-law held down by burning wood: 'I pulled the wood aside and carried her out of the house,' he said.

Chapter 7

Inglorious Career, Inglorious End

Behind me, in the cold, grey waters of the Kaa Fjord, lies the Tirpitz.
William E. West

On a mild September day in 1944, Squadron Leader George Watson was sitting on the grass in front of a hangar at RAF Benson in Oxfordshire, enjoying a rare day off from operational flying as a photo-reconnaissance pilot. As he reflected on his war since leaving the tranquil surroundings of a flying training school in Derbyshire, his thoughts were interrupted by the sight of a familiar figure approaching. Striding towards him was Wing Commander A.H.W. Ball, DSO, DFC, a man later to rise to the rank of Air Marshall.

'It was about midday when the station commander turned up out of the blue and asked if I'd be interested in a special mission. I would have to join up with 617 and 9 Squadrons, who were flying Lancasters. It turned out that they were going to have another go at the *Tirpitz*. My job would be to confirm that the weather conditions were good enough for the raid to go ahead.'

Watson, a native of Alford, Lincolnshire, had wanted to fly ever since he could remember, and in 1936 he joined the RAF Volunteer Reserve and was taught to fly at Woodley, near Reading:

'In those days we were a territorial outfit and, strictly speaking, were full-time civilian flying instructors. I was working as a flying instructor at Waltham in Lincolnshire, but that operation was closed down and everything moved to Burnaston, near Derby. I arrived there in September 1939, just after the outbreak of the war, and we were immediately called up. It was three months, though, before we were given uniforms. In the meantime it was blazers and grey flannels.'

After two years at Burnaston, Watson was posted to operational flying with a meteorological squadron based in Norfolk: 'We flew high-level Spitfires. Our job was to go out over enemy territory to see if the weather was fit for Bomber Command to do their job.'

From Norfolk, Watson found himself posted to 540 Squadron, which, although part of Coastal Command, was based inland at RAF Benson:

'We flew Mosquitoes and were a PRU – a photo-reconnaissance unit. We had two main roles. The first was to photograph potential targets for Bomber Command. The second was to revisit the area after the raids to see what damage had been done. It could be pretty hairy work and my motto was: "Get in, get on, get out." Sometimes we'd be given high priority jobs – targets that we just had to photograph at almost any cost– and we called those "dicers". But I survived. I suppose it was a mixture of good fortune and experience. Don't forget, I was ten years older than most of the other pilots and I'd been flying long before the war.'

Throughout the war, Allied air and naval forces had attempted to sink the *Tirpitz*, the German capital ship that, without even weighing anchor, posed a huge threat to the Arctic convoy routes that were a vital supply line between the Western Allies and the Soviet Union. *Tirpitz* – 52,600 tons (53,444 tonnes) when fully loaded, and with a crew of 2,600 men – had been commissioned at Wihelmshaven in February 1941 and was the flagship of Germany's Baltic Fleet. Her sister ship, the *Bismarck*, had been found and sunk by the Royal Navy in the North Atlantic in May 1941, but *Tirpitz* proved elusive.

In January 1942, *Tirpitz* sailed to Norwegian waters, where she was to spend the rest of the war. The mighty battleship anchored first at Trondheim, and, on 30–31 January, seven British Stirlings of 15 Squadron attempted to attack her in Faettenfjord but failed to locate her. In March, returning to Trondheim from an aborted operation to intercept British convoys, *Tirpitz* came under air attack for the first time when 12 Albacore torpedo biplanes of 817 and 832 Squadrons from the carrier HMS *Victorious* swooped down on her. The battleship avoided all the torpedoes and shot down two Albacores. By the afternoon, *Tirpitz* was safely anchored in Vestfjord, near Narvik.

A few days later, she returned to Trondheim and, within two weeks, was under attack again, this time from thirty-three Halifax bombers. Again the raid was unsuccessful, and six aircraft failed to return. There were two attempts in April. Yet again *Tirpitz* was not hit, and the RAF lost a further seven aircraft. Her sinking was becoming something of an obsession for the Allies, although she never actually came into contact with any Allied shipping and had fired her guns at enemy targets only once, during an Allied raid on shore facilities at Spitsbergen in September 1943.

That month, three British midget submarines in Kaa Fjord attacked her. Two mines, each of 2 tons (1.8 tonnes), were placed under the battleship's keel, and at last *Tirpitz* was seriously damaged. She was out of action for the next six months. One German sailor lost his life and forty of his crewmates were wounded. The three midget submarines were all sunk.

Fully repaired, however, she became a priority target once more. In February 1944, she was attacked, without success, by four Soviet bombers. In April, forty carrier-based British bombers hit her fourteen times, killing 132 of her crew and wounding 316. In August, Barracudas from Royal Navy carriers managed three separate raids on *Tirpitz*. They hit her twice, but there was no serious damage.

The RAF now turned to a new weapon, the Tallboy bomb designed by Barnes Wallis, inventor of the 'bouncing bomb' for the Dambusters. Each Tallboy weighed 12,000lb (5,400kg), had 5,200lb (2,359kg) of high explosive, and was designed for accurate flight and great penetration.

The first major hurdle was that Kaa Fjord in Northern Norway, where *Tirpitz* lay, was well out of return range of Lancasters flying from Britain and carrying Tallboy bombs. It was decided that both 617 Squadron, 'The Dambusters', and 9 Squadron would fly to a base in Yagodnik, an island airfield in Northern Russia, refuel, and carry out the attack from there.

Enter Squadron Leader George Watson. A few days after his daydreams were interrupted at RAF Benson, he was flying from a remote Soviet naval airfield in northern Russian. Finding that airfield in the first place, in the flat, featureless Russian landscape, was no easy task. Several Lancasters had already missed the landing strip and were now stuck in marshy ground. Nearing his destination, Watson had to locate the log cabin 'city' of Archangel, by which time the cloud base was so low that he was flying at rooftop level.

'I was at about 27,000ft [8.23m] and saw a huge weather front ahead, so I decided to keep it visual. It's a good job there weren't any tall buildings in Archangel because I was down to 300ft [91m]. We'd been told to find a lake to the north-west of Archangel and fly around that, otherwise we would be shot at. We'd also been told to make radio contact, but there was a problem with the Russian radio transmitter.

'I also had a problem in that my navigator, Mac, who was a lovely man but wasn't very good at map-reading. I never did find the lake, but I followed the River Dvina and eventually we were on the ground at Yagodnik. It was a godforsaken place, just a few wooden bungalow-type buildings. Someone, though, had thoughtfully hung out a banner proclaiming: "Welcome to the Glorious British Fliers".'

By this time, Watson had yet another problem. An abscess on his left hand had become poisoned, which meant that he would have to make the 1,300-mile (2,292km) round trip to find *Tirpitz* virtually one-handed: 'I hadn't got any choice. I was the only Mosquito pilot for thousands of miles.'

Watson went out every day looking for a break in the weather over *Tirpitz*.

'I couldn't get too near because the Germans would have been alerted, but on about the fourth day the weather cleared a little and I thought the bombers could go in. The timing was so critical that I hadn't got time to land and report in – and there was still no radio contact. So I dived low over the airfield to signal "go", and the Lancasters were taking off before I landed.'

On 15 September 1944, twenty-seven Lancasters, carrying twenty Tallboys, set off at George Watson's signal. With the Lancasters' approach screened by mountains, the Germans were taken by surprise, and *Tirpitz* was late in getting her smokescreens up. One Tallboy smashed straight through *Tirpitz's* forecastle and burst deep in her hull. The shock waves from this bomb, and from near misses, also damaged the ship's engines.

From one of the Lancasters, William E. West, a war correspondent working for the Exchange Telegraph news agency, reported, 'Two squadrons of Lancasters of Bomber Command have just dropped their bombs … Black and orange clouds are rising over the dull, brown smokescreen which was put up over the battleship as we raced in to attack.

'My Lancaster, "L" for London, carried cameras not bombs. The attack was sudden and spectacular. Calculations by meteorological officers and a reconnaissance flight by a Mosquito early in the morning indicated that the weather would be suitable for precision bombing. Pilots and ground crews gave us a great send-off as the bombers lifted their heavy loads. It was a piece of cake in RAF language – until we neared the target … Wing Commander [later Group Captain] W. Tait, DSO and two bars, and DFC, said at the briefing, "You must keep absolutely straight and level for the bombing run. We have not come all this way to drop our bombs in the ruddy fjord." He led the attack himself … It was impossible to mistake the *Tirpitz*. A massive bulk, surrounded by ships and other craft. The smokescreen was already going up as the Germans tried to draw a veil over the nakedness of their greatest warship. From that moment it was a race between the smokescreen and the Lancasters …

Bombs rained down. There was only medium flak, and no fighters. After a minute or two, a great cloud of black smoke billowed up through the brown vapour, and dull orange tints like blanketed flames, also appeared ... The whole attack was over in a few minutes.'

(Seven months later, 35-year-old William E. West was killed by a Japanese sniper in Burma.)

All the Lancasters returned safely to Yagodnik, but George Watson was already back over the target.

'I'd just got back from flying 650 miles [1,046km] there and 650 miles back, most of it one-handed, and the CO said: "Do you think you could go again?" I asked my navigator: "What do you think Mac? Can we go again?" He just shrugged and grunted: "I suppose so."

'This time we had to assess the damage and, of course, apart from having to go in much closer, the Germans were expecting us. When we got over the *Tirpitz*, the weather had closed in again and it was impossible to take any useful pictures. So I decided to find a hole in the cloud, go down and have a look. I spiralled the aircraft down and Mac tried to make an assessment. I'd never seen so much flak before, and I never saw as much again. I read later that there were forty-five heavy gun emplacements around the *Tirpitz*. It felt as if every one of them was shooting at me.'

After the raid, the Germans decided to move *Tirpitz* south, to a shallow berth near Tromso, where she could act as a floating battery. The Allies, however, were still unsure of how successful the Tallboy raid had been – naval intelligence still regarded her as a possible threat to shipping – and the RAF mounted two more raids. In October, little further damage was done to the battleship, but, on 12 November 1944, *Tirpitz* was hit again by Lancasters from 617 and 9 Squadrons, and, as the result of an internal explosion, the mighty battleship rolled over to port and capsized with the loss of almost 1,000 lives. Less than 100 of her crew were rescued.

The naval correspondent of the *Lancashire Daily Post* reported:

'The biggest battleship in the world, *Tirpitz*, has met with an inglorious end after an inglorious career ... She never fought at sea like *Bismarck*, her sister ship.'

On 14 November, the German News Agency broke its silence on *Tirpitz*, reporting that she had been 'put out of action' after an attack by 'super heavy bombers':

> 'The battleship *Tirpitz* was used for the protection of the Northern Norwegian coast, and has repulsed a number of strong enemy air attacks. A great number of British bombers were shot down during these attacks. On Sunday, the battleship was lying in shallow water close to the Norwegian coast when she was attacked by British planes which resulted in the ship being put out of action. The greater part of the crew was saved.'

A German document found after the war confirmed that the September raid in which George Watson had played such a key role had already done the job. It was estimated that repairs, even if they could have been carried out without interruption, would take at least nine months. On 23 September 1944, it was eventually decided that it was no longer possible to make *Tirpitz* ready for sea and action again. Hitler had lost the last influential ship of his surface battlefleet, effectively marking the end of Germany's naval war.

For his part in Operation Paravane – the codename of the September raid on *Tirpitz* – Squadron Leader George Watson was awarded the DFC. He was demobbed in December 1945. Just before he died, in 2006, he said, 'Why did I get involved in flying all those years ago? I don't really know. Because I was a bit stupid I suppose.'

Chapter 8

No Colour Bar In This Country …

The English were not that way. They appreciated us. They treated us royally.
Evelyn Martin-Johnson, Mail handler,
6888th Central Postal Directory Battalion

On Thursday, 5 October 1944, the village of Kingsclere, on the Hampshire-Berkshire border, was the scene of an incident that threatened to sour the vital wartime relationship between Britain and the United States. At the end of that autumn evening, three people – a black GI, a black military policeman (MP) and a 64-year-old local white woman – lay dead after a desire for revenge had spilled over into an act of violence worthy of a Hollywood western.

The men of 3247 Quartermaster Service Company had recently arrived at their new barracks at Sydmonton Court, a country house that stood 3 miles (4.8km) from Kingsclere, in a 5,000-acre estate. Around 7pm, a number of the men, all of whom were black, were drinking at the Bolton Arms pub in Kingsclere when they were challenged by US MPs, also black, who ordered them to return to camp because they had no passes and were improperly dressed in field jackets. Those with drinks were first permitted to finish them. On their way back to Sydmonton Court, the GIs debated what action to take. Several elected to collect their guns and return to the village. At least one, Private Coleman Binns, suspecting 'trouble', decided to go to bed.

The rest arrived back in Kingsclere at around 9.30pm and began to search for the MPs, first at the Bolton Arms where, according to two witnesses – one civilian and one from their own company – the men were carrying arms. Then to the Swan, where they asked after the MPs. They finally found them at the Crown. The GIs took up positions behind the low churchyard wall just across the street. A quiet English village was about to take on the appearance of the American Wild West.

Inside, 'time' had just been called and, as approximately eight other soldiers and several locals quietly downed their drinks and finished games of bar billiards and shove-halfpenny, two of the MPs stepped outside. A single shot was heard, followed almost immediately by a fusillade of bullets. One of the MPs, Private Jacob J. Anderson, despite being hit in the chest, managed to stagger away; his colleague scrambled back inside the pub and took cover with other drinkers and staff who were cowering under tables and behind bars as bullets spattered against the stucco front of the building, leaving some thirty or so bullet marks on its walls and on those of two nearby homes. Other bullets went through the windows, and, as he dived for cover, Private Joseph Coates, who had been sitting with his back to the window of the smoking room, was killed instantly by a shot that fractured his skull and lacerated his brain.

When the shooting had started, landlady Rose Napper had been pulled to the ground by her husband, Frank. She was hit by a ricocheting bullet that passed through her left cheek, through her tongue and out through the right of her neck. Despite valiant efforts to save her, she died in hospital just before 5am the following day. Others received minor injuries from bullets, broken glass and splintering shrapnel. By the time the police arrived, the perpetrators had fled. Two local women, returning from their own night out, found Private Anderson as he lay dying in a front garden some 500ft (150m) from the Crown. The bullet had gone through his right lung and penetrated the pulmonary artery. He was suffocating in his own blood.

At around 3am, police captured the first of the suspects, who was taken back to the Crown to be questioned. The others were identified and charged over the following few days, while the residents of Kingsclere struggled to comprehend what had happened in their quiet, picturesque village.

Despite the crimes taking place on British soil, and one of the victims being a British citizen, there was to be no public trial in a British court. Instead, ten men – Privates Ernest Burn, Willie J. Crawford, Hildreth H. Fleming snr, Herbert Lawton, Herbert Moultrie, Percy D. Oree, Privates 1st Class James L. Agnew, John E. Lockett, Willie Washington and Corporal John W. Lilly – faced a US court martial, which was held in a mess hall. The *Newbury Weekly News* reported on the proceedings. There were written statements from most defendants who either did not know who fired the shots or who admitted firing over the roof of the pub. Several said they had been drinking, or that they had dived for cover when the shooting began. Together their statements painted a complex picture, although they all agreed that, when they set out, they had not intended to harm anyone. They merely wanted to speak with the MPs.

Only Private Crawford chose to give evidence in person. He said that he had joined the group on their way back to Kingsclere and that he had left his weapon behind (this was confirmed by his CO's evidence). After some cross-examination, Crawford reluctantly pointed the finger squarely at two of his comrades who he had heard discussing the idea of killing 'that MP'.

The prosecution pointed out that, under US military code, there was no difference between an 'accessory after the fact' and the 'principal' and that evidence showed that some members of the group intended to commit murder, and that the entire group joined in, putting them all in the frame.

Nine of the men – even Crawford, who had been unarmed – were found guilty of murder, riotous assembly and being absent without leave. The cause of their initial anger was never revealed. All the men were dishonourably discharged. They were sentenced to life imprisonment with hard labour, to be served in the United States. Even the remaining defendant, Lawton, found guilty of being absent without leave for just thirty minutes, was sentenced to ten years' hard labour. The rest of the 3247 Quartermaster Service Company were hastily moved overseas. Although the incident was reported locally, there was minimal national coverage. There is no doubt that it was played down, 'hushed up', even. On General Eisenhower's order, an apology was given to the village and the risk of a compromised relationship between the Allies was averted.

What happened at Kingsclere could not have been anticipated by the authorities in either Britain or the United States. What was anticipated, at least in Britain, was the kind of cultural clash in which more than two million American troops, many of whom came from states where racial segregation was enshrined in law, were deposited in, or passed through, a country where segregation had never been practised. Specifically, the British authorities were concerned what might happen when British citizens witnessed the way that many white GIs treated their black compatriots. For that reason, the Government requested that the United States limit the number of black GIs posted to Britain. The United States refused, and approximately 10 per cent (200,000) of the GIs stationed in Britain were African-Americans. Significantly, almost none of them were officers, and few were MPs, the Kingsclere business being a rare exception.

The Government remained worried. What would happen in an English village should the United States decide to try to impose their own segregation laws? What would happen if the generally fair-minded British public saw black GIs being treated unjustly? And how would white American GIs react if they witnessed locals showing kindness to 'coloureds'?

There was also the sticky situation of how to handle any tensions that might arise should white GIs encounter black troops from the British Empire. Britain was in a unique position because it enjoyed the support of its colonies and was keen to avoid anything that might threaten that. At least one such incident did come to the attention of the Foreign Office, who considered it serious enough to present a report to the US charge d'affaires.

Britain desperately needed US assistance. That Britain would adopt American-style segregation was out of the question, but the Government essentially avoided forming any specific policy on the issue. The absence of any official guidance left a vacuum into which individuals issued their own local guidance on how to behave. In August 1942, Major General Arthur Dowler, at the time in charge of the administration of Southern Command, issued his 'Notes on relations with Coloured Troops'. These were supposedly intended for limited distribution, but soon became widely available. Even in 1940s Britain, his words were controversial; to modern Britons they are outright offensive:

'While there are many coloured men of high mentality and cultural distinction, the generality are of a simple mental outlook. They work hard when they have no money and when they have money prefer to do nothing until it is gone. In short, they do not have the white man's ability to think and act to a plan. Their spiritual outlook is well known, and their songs give the clue to their nature ... Too much freedom, too wide associations with white men tend to make them lose their heads and have on occasions led to civil strife.'

In case a reminder was needed, the following month F.A. Newsome of the Home Office issued the following advice to chief constables across the nation:

'It is not the policy of His Majesty's Government that any discrimination as regards the treatment of coloured troops should be made by the British authorities. The Secretary of State, therefore, would be glad if you would be good enough to take steps to ensure that the police do not make any approach to the proprietors of public houses, restaurants, cinemas, or other places of entertainment with a view to discriminating against coloured troops.'

The Cabinet remained split on the issue. Sir James Grigg, Secretary of State for War, issued a memorandum 'suggesting that Army personnel should be educated to adopt towards coloured troops the attitude adopted by the United States Army authorities'. In contrast, Minister of Information Brendon Bracken wrote an article in the *Sunday Express* noting that the 'Colour Bar must go'.

Finally, a sort of non-policy was fudged together by Sir Stafford Cripps, the Lord Privy Seal, who drew up a document entitled: 'United States Negro Troops in the United Kingdom', to be circulated to senior officers in the Army and RAF:

'In the South [of the United States] the white population still tend to regard Negroes as children for whom they have a moral responsibility; like children, Negroes commonly inspire affection and admiration; but they are not considered "equal" to white men and women any more than children are considered equal to adults … it is not for us to embarrass them [the Americans], even if we have different views on how race relationships should be treated in our own country and in the Empire … there is no reason why British soldiers and auxiliaries should adopt the American attitude but they should respect it and avoid making it a subject for argument and dispute.'

Cripps's advice, as well meaning as it probably was, brushed over entirely the ingrained, and often brutal, racism enshrined in law across vast swathes of the United States. A racism that was deep-rooted, and not about to be put to one side just because black and white were fighting a war against a common enemy. His words did nothing to prevent conflict between white and black servicemen. Or the incidents of violence. Some of which resulted in more death and injury.

Tensions with black troops stationed around the Lancashire village of Bamber Bridge had been high since US commanders there had, against the wishes of locals, attempted to racially segregate pubs. News from home, where race riots had broken out, made matters worse. In June 1943, a row had begun when US MPs attempted to arrest one of a group of black soldiers from 1511 Quartermaster Truck Regiment for being 'out of uniform' while drinking at Ye Olde Hob Inn. Several locals, including British service personnel, had stood up for the soldier, and the MPs had left the pub. But, as they left, someone threw a glass of beer at their jeep. The MPs reported to base where they were ordered to return, with reinforcements, and arrest the soldiers. The black GIs were making their way back to their own barracks when the MPs found them. A fight started and a shot rang out – one of the MPs had fatally wounded Private William Crossland. The GIs, some of them carrying injuries, returned to barracks where the unit's only black officer persuaded the men that their acting CO would round up the MPs involved and see that justice was done. However, around midnight, several jeeploads of MPs, heavily armed, including at least one large machine gun, were seen in the area. A rumour spread that the MPs were searching for black soldiers to shoot and matters rapidly escalated. The GIs took two-thirds of the rifles from the barracks and set off to find the MPs. As they searched, they were ambushed at an MP roadblock.

With locals warned to stay inside, a firefight continued for several hours. When it ended, at 4am, seven men had been wounded – an officer, three black GIs and one MP by gunshot, and two MPs beaten up. Thirty-two black soldiers were convicted of mutiny. However, the racist attitudes of the MPs, and poor leadership, were cited as causes. Ultimately, even the lengthiest sentences (seven men sentenced to more than twelve years' imprisonment) were reduced. The longest term served was thirteen months, and most of the men were quickly returned to duty. Across the US Army, attempts were made to weed-out the worst of the racist officers and to improve the quality of commanders of black units. This reduced the severity and frequency of such conflicts, but segregation continued.

In the Bristol area, some 300,000 US servicemen had almost doubled the local population. Black and white troops were billeted separately. Living conditions varied greatly – with the lower quality billets always being assigned to black soldiers. Their working hours tended to be longer, too. The US military in Bristol decided to maintain segregation during off-duty hours, but they could not divide an entire city into separate halves and, with so many troops, and facilities squashed into a relatively confined area, absolute segregation was impractical. At one pub, the Colston Arms – ironically named after Bristol's most notorious slave owner – after the US military attempted to prevent black GIs from entering, Bristolians fought back. Colston Arms regulars posted a 'Black Troops Only' sign on the pub's door.

In Bristol, black and white troops had separate Red Cross centres, but they were less than a quarter of a mile (400m) apart. In the summer of 1944, tensions grew. On 10 July, black GIs billeted at the Muller Orphanage accused white paratroopers of insulting and beating them. Two days later and some 3 miles (4.8km) away in the suburb of Sea Mills, 545 Port Company refused to report for duty, demanding better treatment from officers, improved accommodation and an end to white paratroopers pursuing black soldiers through the streets of the city. The mutiny ended that evening, without violence, although the soldier identified as being responsible for organising the protest was sentenced to hard labour for life. On Saturday, 15 July, 400 black GIs gathered in the area of Park Street and Great George Street. Many of them were in the company of local white women. When the soldiers tried to enter local pubs, white American MPs prevented them. There was a stand-off, with locals cheering on the black troops. A minor fracas resulted in the deployment of more MPs, bringing the total to 120. An attempt was made to force the troops back to barracks and some MPs demanded that several soldiers hand over the knives they were carrying. When they refused, more MPs and more GIs became involved.

In the confrontation that followed, one policeman was stabbed, and his attacker shot dead. To restore control, the MPs used buses to close off the street, and opened fire, shooting several GIs in their legs. There followed many arrests and a curfew, which lasted for several days. To avoid a repeat, US authorities decided to drastically reduce the number of its troops stationed in the area.

The previous month had seen a fracas in the West Midlands town of Dudley. Trouble had started inside the Mirabelle Dance Hall when a black soldier had taken exception to a white comrade dancing with 'his girl'. The manager, Mr J. Gibson, had overheard the argument and cast the pair out into the street. There a fight began involving a number of each man's friends, and several suffered minor injuries. As the confrontation grew – more and more soldiers were joining in – it spread through the centre of the town. Again, shots were fired, and the disturbance continued through the night until MPs managed to restore order.

In general, though, when it came to relations between black GIs and British citizens, there was mutual respect. There were conflicts, of course. For example, some business owners did shy away from outwardly welcoming new black customers because, as one restaurant manager had told African-American journalist Roi Ottley, 'White Americans say they will not patronise my place if Negroes are served'. And, in August 1943, Learie Constantine, the famous Trinidadian cricketer, finding his family's hotel reservation cut short at the insistence of white American servicemen, successfully sued the hotel responsible. Constantine had also had an ugly encounter with an USAF officer at a dance hall on Merseyside. The cricketer, already a household name, held back the desire to strike the American who had called him a 'nigger' and instead handed him over to the hall's porter who ejected him. Had he struck the airman, said Constantine, he knew that the resultant newspaper headlines would have further inflamed 'the black and white problem … with England at that time filled with black and white American troops'.

Most Britons, however, welcomed black GIs with open arms and warmth and, as the British authorities had suspected, were utterly blindsided by the terrible treatment of black people by many white Americans in the military. Many was the occasion when locals defended the black personnel against racism, something which often neither resolved nor diffused matters. In a Southend-on-Sea hotel when six white sailors attacked a black comrade, simply because he was dancing with a white girl, locals tried, but failed, to prevent this. The dance was still cancelled because most of the young women were so appalled by his treatment that they refused to dance with any of the hundred or so white troops. Mark Mendoza, who had witnessed the scene with his family, wrote to Anthony Eden to express his anger: 'I am particularly disgusted that at this point of the war when so many men are dying in the fight for the rights of mankind, this sort of persecution should be allowed a free hand in our liberty loving Empire.' He was not alone, although many preferred to leave the Foreign Secretary to his own devices and write to the newspapers instead.

The Ministry of Information's Home Intelligence Division produced weekly reports into all aspects of public morale.

'Discrimination against their coloured brethren by white US soldiers has been criticised consistently ... The "colour bar" is criticised as being undemocratic and as "conflicting with the Englishman's idea of fair play".'

Gunner Mostyn Jones, for example, wrote an impassioned counter-argument to a letter published in the *Pontypridd Observer* from 'An Airman in India', complaining about the 'introduction of American coloured soldiers into Pontypridd's social life'. Jones declared:

'He hardly wants to return to a country where women have sunk to the level of accepting the advances of coloured men ... I hardly want to return to a country – the home of a man who has sunk to the level of accepting the arrogant doctrine of racial superiority practised by the Fascists who we are fighting to liquidate.'

S.E. Lewsley, writing to the *Lincolnshire Echo*, was one of several drawing similar comparisons after emergency accommodation had not been made available to coloured soldiers: 'It would appear that one has no need to visit the totalitarian countries to find dictatorship or racial prejudice.'

In Bath, where one pub banned black servicemen to appease their white comrades, dozens of appalled citizens wrote to the local newspaper to object, one noting: 'These men have been sent to this country to help in its defence, and whatever their race or creed they should be entitled to the same treatment as our own soldiers.'

Some citizens went further than letter writing. J. Lebolo-Carey, in the London *Daily News*, reported:

'Two coloured American soldiers got on a Cardiff tram. Two [white] American officers followed, and one told the coloured soldiers to "Get out". As they were about to leave, the conductress stopped them. "You are in Britain. Coloured men are not banned from our cars. Stay on." And they stayed put. When the officers were getting off they said: "You English [sic] are making it hard for us; when we get back to America, we shall not be able to manage these fellows."

Indeed, it has been suggested that the positive way the British treated American black servicemen during the war was a factor in the US Civil Rights Movement that followed.

One letter, this time in the *Diss Express*, came from a correspondent signing themselves as 'FAIR PLAY FOR ALL' and voiced anger

'that in a certain village in East Anglia certain white American soldiers objected to coloured soldiers dancing with white girls. I think this is, sir, quite a question for the white girls to decide for themselves. Whatever the American does in his own country, he certainly does not rule our social life here; and in many cases the manner and behaviour of the coloured soldiers are to be preferred to those of some of the white American soldiers.'

The Home Intelligence Division had found evidence to support this, reporting frequently on Britons' gratitude for 'the extremely pleasing manners of the coloured troops'. One letter, written by a canteen worker in Hull, was intercepted while being checked by the ministry's postal censors and read:

'We find the coloured troops are much nicer to deal with ... they're always so courteous and have a very natural charm that most of the whites miss ... I'd far rather serve [them] than a couple of whites ... All my friends – most of them were colour conscious before – who serve in canteens feel the same.'

And George Orwell noted that 'the general consensus of opinion is that the only American soldiers with decent manners are Negroes'.

Most Britons' interactions with black troops were entirely positive. For most, other than those living in the busy port cities, these were the first non-white people they had ever encountered. Some trepidation was to be expected, but integration and harmony abounded. In many cases, black GIs joined in with their British hosts in local events, helping in emergencies like shovelling snow and helping to get supplies to villages cut off by inclement weather. They found particular common ground when it came to matters of faith.

In Ballymena, County Antrim, where the local Methodist church was holding a special evening choral service, a large congregation, led by Reverend R.J. Black, was treated to the singing of a choir of black soldiers, led by Sergeant Myles. According to the *Ballymena Daily Telegraph*, the choir 'rendered several sacred songs and spirituals'.

In Bootle, in the spring of 1945, black US troops joined the family, teachers and classmates at the funeral of 9-year-old Rebecca Sanders. The GIs had formed a close bond with the little girl as she had passed by their guard post on her way to and from Gray Street Council School. With her parents' permission, she had repeatedly visited them 'because they are lonely and like to talk to me about their home'. So beloved was young Rebecca that, as soon as they learned she had been admitted to hospital, the troops had sent her books, sweets and oranges. After her death, the soldiers 'filed bareheaded past the little coffin'. The little girl had made such an impact in her short life that every one of her fifty classmates had written letters of condolence, and the curtains of every neighbour's, as well as those at the guard post, were drawn on the day of the funeral. Rebecca's family were much touched by the soldiers' tribute to their young friend, her father telling the *Liverpool Post* 'The American soldiers could not possibly have done more than they did.'

Sir Stafford Cripps had warned that 'for a white woman to go about in the company of a Negro American is likely to lead to controversy and ill-feeling, it may also be misunderstood by the Negro troops themselves. This does not mean that friendly hospitality in the home or in social gatherings need be ruled out, though in such cases care should be taken not to invite white and coloured American troops at the same time'.

If Cripps's judgement on the black GIs themselves was unfair, his overall concerns were not so wide of the mark. Romantic relationships between white British women and black GIs did prove one of the most contentious elements of the GI 'invasion' of Britain. Understandably, given the absence of many British men from their hometowns and the presence of thousands of confident, young Americans, equipped with plentiful and hard-to-find treats of chocolate and nylons, many women and girls enjoyed the company of GIs whether black or white.

Not all liaisons were about finding long-term companionship, and many were not of a romantic nature at all. And they were more likely to make the pages of newspapers, particularly if they offered the additional novelty of involving black GIs. In August 1944, readers of the *Derby Evening Telegraph* learned about two twenty-something women 'of no fixed address' who had been discovered by local policemen – one 'wandering around Derby bus station', the other on 'Bass's Recreation Ground' in the town centre. Both admitted 'spending the night in the fields with coloured soldiers'. This relative lack of sensationalism was hardly surprising given that, throughout history, wherever troops, with money in their pockets, had gathered, it was common to find women who lived on the edge of society.

Those who disapproved of any friendly relationship between black and white found ways to be heard. Like the one played out in the West Country village of Worle, near Weston-super-Mare. Mrs May, wife of the local vicar, gave a talk unveiling a six-point plan to be enacted should 'American coloured troops' ever be sent to the village. Her proposals were designed to prevent scandal should local white women and black GIs ever mix, but they 'amazed' the other villagers. Mrs May advised female shopkeepers to serve a black GI as quickly as possible, and 'indicate that she does not desire him to come there again … if she is in a shop and a coloured soldier comes in, she leaves as soon as she has made her purchase or before that if she is in a queue'. Mrs May also suggested that, if at the cinema, a black soldier should sit beside her, a white woman should change seats and should also cross the road to avoid passing by a black soldier at close quarters.

'White women must have no social relationship with coloured troops … on no account must coloured troops be invited into the homes of white women'.

Mrs May told her audience not to repeat her talk to the newspapers in case it 'hurt the coloured troops'. One unnamed local woman said, 'I was disgusted, and so were most of the women there. We have no intention of agreeing to her decree.'

Many were so disgusted that they told their husbands, one of whom was a local councillor who reported it to the Ministry of Information. The *Sunday Pictorial* assured black GIs, 'Any coloured soldier who reads this may rest assured that there is no colour bar in this country and that he is as welcome as any other Allied Soldier. He will find that the vast majority of people here have nothing but repugnance for the narrow-minded, uninformed prejudices expressed by the vicar's wife. There is – and will be – no persecution of coloured people in Britain.'

Eventually there were other, very visible, complications of love affairs to take into consideration. It is estimated that some 2,000 so-called 'brown babies' were born to white British women and black GIs during the war. The Home Intelligence Report noted that the main concern was that almost all these children were born 'illegitimate'. In fact, this could not be avoided. All American servicemen had to receive permission to marry from their commanding officer or risk a court martial. In thirty of the forty-eight states (at the time), mixed-raced marriages were outlawed and barely any black GIs wishing to marry were granted permission.

In November 1944, the director of the American Red Cross Club in Derby informed the local Borough Social Welfare Committee that 'American coloured soldiers are seeking legal aid in a desire to create a trust fund for coloured babies in the nursery at Boundary House'. The Boundary House Institution looked after Derby's poor and needy and ran a number of small children's homes across the town. Its nursery was based in the Institution's headquarters – known until 1930 as the Derby Poor Law Union Workhouse. The town's council debated a resolution urging the British and American governments to collaborate on the establishments of hostels that could care for the illegitimate children of black soldiers and white British women to ensure that 'children whose fathers are American soldiers should be given an equal opportunity in life with other children'.

One councillor, G.A. Collier, objected, apparently believing the babies' mixed heritage was heavily weighted in favour of their fathers' and that, therefore, they belonged to the United States: 'The resolution should take steps to have these children sent back to the States among their own people when the war is over. I feel they would have a better deal there.'

The Mayor, Councillor William H. Phillips, however, believed firmly that the responsibility for them lay with their mothers' country. Councillor A.J. Luckett, who had proposed the resolution, noted that, although dark-skinned children might be unusual in the town, they were, above all else, human beings and ought to be treated as such.'

The arrival of non-white troops in the Derby area had caused some needless friction. In August 1997, Elsie Church told her grandson, Peter King, 'In Derby when the Americans came, the black Americans came, and the white Americans came. In Derby they had separate nights for them both to be out. They never let both the black and the white Americans in town together, because there was still a bit of tension. They were lovely boys the black boys were. You had nothing to be afraid of. They were good lads.'

If these new complications caused the nation to have uncomfortable conversations, there seemed to be one matter upon which almost everyone agreed: prisoners of war ought not to have more rights than black GIs. In Saffron Walden, Essex, where the town council had refused a request from white GIs to enforce their colour bar on the ground that 'those men were fighting on our side', there was little sympathy for Italian POWs confronted by the same GIs. They were barred from attending local cinemas and town hall dances, even though they were permitted to 'wander the streets freely' and seemed to be 'a well-behaved lot'. They were, after all, the 'enemy'.

Chapter 9

When Do We Get Home?

This is undoubtedly the greatest American battle of the war and will, I believe, be regarded as an ever-famous American victory.

Winston Churchill

S *unday Sun* war correspondent J.H. Morgan was one of the first British journalists to break the news. Reporting from SHAEF in Paris on 16 December 1944, Morgan filed his story: 'The Germans launched counterattacks in the Ardennes today. At dawn they struck at widely separated points on a 75-mile front facing the United States First Army ... No further details were available from SHAEF tonight, but earlier reports suggested that the first impact of the attack was met by our troops.'

Ever since the Allies had broken out of Normandy in August, they had faced a hard, grinding slog towards the Rhine, while the Germans had been preparing for a massive counterattack. It came just before Christmas. What Morgan was reporting was the beginning of Operation Wacht Am Rhein ('Watch on the Rhine'), later known as Autumn Mist, or more popularly as the Battle of the Bulge.

The remarkably ill-advised plan by Hitler, who had assumed direct control of Germany's armed forces in December 1941, was opposed by his military leaders, notably by Field Marshals Gerd von Rundstedt and Walter Model. Hitler's aim was to drive a wedge through the Allied armies, cross the River Meuse, retake the deep-water port of Antwerp to prevent supplies coming in and then reach the English Channel. After the Allies had been encircled, said Hitler, then they would be compelled to settle for a peace treaty on Germany's terms, thus releasing German troops to concentrate on defending the east from imminent invasion by the Soviet Union.

Early on that murky winter's morning, more than 200,000 German soldiers and almost 1,000 tanks had launched what would prove to be a last desperate attempt to reverse the Allied successes that had followed D-Day. The battleground Hitler had chosen was densely wooded, served by few roads and held by four American divisions comprising battle-weary troops, many of whom had limited combat experience, and had been put there mainly for rest and recuperation.

The surprise attack gained initial successes, breaking through the front, seizing critical crossroads, isolating one American infantry division and pushing forwards to create the 'bulge' in the Allied line that would give the battle its name.

There was initial confusion among Allied troops and, among a Belgian civilian population that had been celebrating their liberation, sheer chaos and panic ensued. There were reports of German paratroopers dropping behind Allied lines, of English-speaking German soldiers dressed in American uniforms cutting communication lines and capturing key bridges, and, terrifyingly, of soldiers and civilians being murdered. What became known as the 'Malmedy Massacres', a series of summary executions carried out by Waffen SS infantry on American prisoners of war and Belgians alike, would result in war crimes trials that saw forty-three death sentences for those responsible. In one instance alone, eighty-four American soldiers who had surrendered were herded into a farmer's field near the Belgian city of Malmedy and machine-gunned to death or shot through the head. Some forty Americans did survive, either by pretending to be dead or fleeing into surrounding woods as the Germans opened fire.

Over Christmas, improved weather conditions allowed Allied air attacks on German troops and supply lines. It would prove to be the turning point, although, on 27 December, the *Daily Mirror's* David Walker cautioned against taking the outcome for granted:

'Despite Sunday's hammering from the air, when more Allied aircraft were flung into battle than on any other day since the German counterattack began, the Hun has not yet shot his bolt. Over Christmas his thrust merged into a single 40-mile [64km] deep salient and now he is trying hard to break out north and north-west while we still have to keep American troops in Bastogne supplied from the air. On the other hand, lots of small enemy groups are being eliminated … The highlight from our point of view was undoubtedly Sunday, when between 6,000 and 7,000 Allied planes gave German material perhaps its greatest and most shattering blow ever. They left more than 700 smouldering vehicles … Even so, the battle is not yet over, and at this moment more Panzer patrols are still pushing forward like the fingers of a man who has got his foot in the door and is trying for all he's worth to push the door wide open. We can reasonably hope that the worst of this particular push may be over …'

It was. Although they managed to advance for 50 miles (80.4km) in some sectors, the Germans' success was short-lived. Despite suffering heavy losses, the Americans delayed the enemy long enough for reinforcements to arrive and, less than two weeks after the beginning of the counterattack, it was clear that the Germans would fail in their objective. Tanks of General Patton's Third Army had relieved the besieged town of Bastogne – gallantly held by men of the 82nd and 101st Airborne – where all seven main roads through the Ardennes highlands converged. The Americans' resistance denied the Germans use of the Antwerp port. When asked on 22 December to surrender, Bastogne's defender, Brigadier General Antony C. McAuliffe, had famously responded with 'Nuts!'

Into January 1945, incredibly brave and tenacious American soldiers operated in small units and in thick snow and sub-zero temperatures. The US Third Army attacked from the south, its First Army from the north. The UK's 6th Airborne Division, which included 1st Canadian Parachute Battalion, together with the 23rd Hussars and tanks of the Fife and Forfar Yeomanry, were also involved. Elements of the 7th Armoured Division, the 'Desert Rats', who were out on rest, and the 53rd Welsh Infantry Division had also found themselves back in action, helping to cut off the tip of the Germans' northern salient.

On 9 January, Leonard Mosley, who was embedded with the 6th Airborne in the mountains of the Ardennes, painted a vivid picture of what those troops were having to endure: 'All through this cold and bitter winter's day, huddled into my heavy sheepskin jacket and peering through the gently drifting snow, I have been watching a tale of British gallantry and endurance unfolding before my eyes. I have been watching British soldiers fighting and dying in one of the most difficult and heroic actions of the war ... No defender ever had more advantage of weather and conditions and terrain. Yet over this terrible range of mountains, down into those valleys and ravines, a division of British troops have been advancing for more than a week now. By sheer guts and courage and native refusal to be beaten they have relentlessly pressed their way east over the bodies of hundreds of German dead and the frozen bodies of scores of their comrades.'

When the battle was over, of the 55,000 who took part, British and Canadian casualties numbered approximately 1,400 killed, wounded or missing. In contrast, some 600,000 Americans were involved in the Battle of the Bulge, and it was reported that they suffered 89,000 casualties, including around 19,000 killed. Many of the wounded suffered 'cold injuries' – frostbite, trench foot, even pneumonia – in the brutal conditions of record-breaking low temperatures, snow and freezing rain. Some simply froze to death before they could be rescued. American baseball Hall of Famer, Warren Spahn, who served in an Engineer Combat Group, wrote later, 'I was from Buffalo. I thought I knew cold. But I didn't really know cold until the Battle of the Bulge. Our feet were frozen when we went to sleep, and they were frozen when we woke up.'

The Germans lost approximately 100,000 men in the disastrous operation, not to mention losing weapons and other stores that they could not replace. The realisation that the scales could not be turned, and that the Allied advance could not be stopped, had a huge effect on German morale. They would now be in retreat for the remainder of the war.

Winston Churchill was keen that all the credit should be given to the Americans. In a speech to the House of Commons on 18 January, he said,

'I have seen it suggested that the terrific battle which has been proceeding since December 16, on the American front, is an Anglo-American battle. In fact, however, the United States troops have done almost all the fighting and have suffered almost all the losses. Only one single British Army corps has been engaged. All the rest of the thirty or more divisions which have been fighting continuously for the last month are United States troops. They have lost sixty to eighty men for every one of ours … We ourselves, a month or two earlier, lost 40,000 men in opening the Scheldt, but the bulk of our armies, on the occasion when Rundstedt's attacked, was separated by scores of miles from the impact of the new offensive. According to the professional advice I have at my disposal, what was done to meet Rundstedt's counterstroke was resolute, wise and militarily correct. Field Marshall Montgomery and General Omar Bradley handled their forces in a manner which may become a model for the future, and all the troops fought in a magnificent fashion … Let the Germans dismiss from their minds any idea that losses or setbacks of the kind we have witnessed will turn us from our purpose. For myself I do not hesitate today to give my own opinion that the decisive breaking of the German offensive in the West is more likely to shorten the war than to lengthen it. By this violent offensive, which the Germans have lost, they have in no way delayed, still less averted, the doom closing upon them. As I see it, the Germans have made a violent and costly sortie which has been repulsed with heavy slaughter, and they have expended in that endeavour forces which they cannot replace against an enemy which has more than replaced every loss that he has sustained.'

All the territory lost in December had been regained, and the Allied advance towards the Rhine, the last major barrier before the onward march into the heart of Germany, was back on course. The crossing of the Rhine was not only critical in the physical sense, getting over the legendary river would also be a great psychological achievement. It came on 7 March 1945. Cologne was captured on 5 March, and the American 9th Armored Division then found that the Ludendorff railway bridge at Remagan, 34 miles (55km) from Cologne, had survived German efforts to destroy it. The bridge, which had been built during the First World War, came under heavy air and ground artillery attacks. It had already been damaged by German attempts to blow it up, and now overuse, both by the advancing Americans and retreating Germans, had weakened it further. The conversion from a railway bridge to a road bridge had not been ideal either, and, ten days later, it collapsed, killing thirty soldiers. By then, however, thousands of American troops, their tanks and supplies had crossed the Rhine, and Eisenhower declared the bridge at Remagan 'worth its weight in gold'.

On 23 March, Operation Plunder saw Montgomery's 21st Army Group together with American troops cross the Rhine around Wesel, an ancient town in ruins after Allied air raids. Bailey bridges and amphibious landing craft, as well as parachute and glider landings, were involved in several co-ordinated crossings between Wesel and Rees, one of the oldest towns in the lower Rhine area. Operation Varsity was the largest airborne operation undertaken in a single day, with almost 14,000 paratroopers dropped east of the Rhine to take care of German artillery and deepen the Allies' bridgehead. On 25 March, Winston Churchill crossed the Rhine in a 'Higgins boat', an American LCVP (landing craft, vehicle, personnel), setting foot on the eastern bank of the river. It was hugely symbolic. In Montgomery's staff car, he was driven to the railway bridge at Wesel, that was still under enemy fire. Eisenhower said later that, had he been present, he would have prevented such an act.

On the eve of Operation Plunder, the *Hampshire Telegraph* had commented,

'The war goes well. News from all fronts is so good that we no longer talk of duration times of months, but weeks. Even experts agree that it cannot last longer than the early summer, and military opinion points to an overwhelming defeat in the West within a month of the Allies crossing the Rhine on a major scale. Prisoners are streaming in by the thousand, and organised resistance in many sectors is confined to suicide squads. Those Germans still on the west of the Rhine are faced with disaster, enormous toll has been taken of transport fleeing eastwards, and thousands of Huns are doomed to end their days in this last of the Rhine pockets. Great as has been the destruction caused by the Tactical Air Force in this region during the past week, it is but a foretaste of what is coming to the enemy on the east side of the Rhine. First foreign workers were advised to leave Frankfurt and Mannheim, now General Eisenhower has issued another warning to civilians to get out of the Ruhr – and out of the war. These and other unmistakable signs on all sectors of the Rhine front are but preliminaries to the great battle soon to begin.'

The Allies' plans for what they would do with the vanquished Nazi state were already well formed. On the first day of the Battle of the Bulge, Reuters reported that Eisenhower had told the Germans that all Nazi educational organisations would be abolished by the Allies, and the teaching of military subjects forbidden. 'The schools will be re-opened as soon as possible,' he said. 'Every German teacher will receive instructions to avoid teaching military subjects, Nazism, unjust racial treatment and hostility to any of the united Allied nations. Any teacher who disobeys these instructions will be relieved of his post at once and will be liable to severe punishment.' The Third Reich was fast crumbling. 'Young SS men on the Western Front are wantonly destroying German homes and farms – not as part of a deliberate scorched earth policy but from sheer habit. Himmler admits this himself,' wrote Reuters' continental observer.

Tens of thousands of Allied troops now poured over the Rhine. On 31 March 1945, the *Daily Record* proclaimed, '190 Miles From Berlin – Still Going'.

'The Allied steel tide is still surging into the heart of Germany. Spearheading the advance today, US 1st Army troops rolled through Paderborn, key road and rail hub, 58 miles [93km] south-west of Hanover, and 190 miles [305km] from the heart of Berlin – and tonight are still rolling ...'

Victory was in sight, although the *Rochdale Observer* mused on how it would all end:

'Nemesis. These are dramatic days. The victory over Germany for which we have worked and endured for five and a half grim years, is now all but complete ... We are in process of witnessing the greatest disaster that has overtaken any nation in the world's history. Nemesis has never acted more completely. We are all wondering how the end will actually come ... But on the whole it has been apparent that the German army has lost the will to fight, and resistance inspired only by the desire for self-preservation has been overcome by British and American troops whose morale has never been higher. Their task is almost complete.'

Reuters correspondent Charles Lynch said that there were two questions in the mind of the British spearhead soldier: 'When will it end?' and 'When do we get home?' Lynch could answer only in part: 'There is reason to believe that the answer to the question "When will it end?" is already fixed, and the date set on which the war will be declared over; but it may be months before there is even a hint of an answer to the soldier's question "When do we get home?"'

Chapter 10

The Battle of the Flying Bombs

The spirit of Londoners remained staunch, asking no diversion of Allied strength to deal with the flying-bomb coast.

Lord Woolton, Minister of Reconstruction

On 13 May 1944, the *Daily News* carried a report about a 'pilotless German plane which crashed in South Sweden'. It was believed to be 'one of the radio-controlled jet-propelled "flying bombs" with which German engineers were reported to be experimenting last year on the Baltic island of Bornholm'. The doodlebugs, as they become known, would soon be on their way to terrorise the civilian population of England.

'Was it a secret weapon?' asked the *Aberdeen Press and Journal*. Of the object that had crashed at the pretty village of Kivik in neutral Sweden, no sign of engine parts or crew had been found, nor any fire or trace of petrol, and witnesses quoted in the Swedish Press described a sound 'not unlike an aeroplane motor, but much louder'. The Free Danish Press Service reported that the machine was 6–8yd (5.4m to 7.3m) long and shaped liked a bomb, but equipped with ailerons like stabilisers. All that was known was that the Germans had been experimenting with radio-controlled 'rocket bombs' on Bornholm in occupied Demark, only 30 miles (48km) from Kivik.

The answer came, in part, from Stockholm, where Edwin Kirchoff, a German Overseas New Agency correspondent, said that German combat aircraft were being held back to strike against invading Allied troops. He described them as having almost unbelievable speed in diving and being 'equipped with weapons so far unknown to the British and the Americans'. Other Axis commentators hinted at German defensive 'surprises'. Reuters quoted a warning from Admiral Alfred Saalweachter, the German Overseas New Agency's naval correspondent:

'On land and in the air, the Germans have a few surprises in store for the invading army. The time has not yet come to say more about this, but the Anglo-American invasion, which will no doubt bring many feints, will be up against many surprises.'

The V-weapons ('V' for Vergeltungswaffen or vengeance, retaliatory) had begun development in the early 1940s. In September 1943, Albert Speer, the Nazi Minister of Armaments and War Production, had promised retribution for the mass bombing of German cities by the RAF. It would be a secret weapon, he said. Since October 1943, missile sites had been going up along the French coast from Le Havre to Calais. In June 1944, the Reich Propaganda Ministry announced the 'Vergeltungswaffen 1' guided missile. According to local legend, just before midnight on 29 May 1944, a missile fired from France landed on Sarisbury Green, a small community close to Farnham in Hampshire. There was no newspaper report to back up the claim, but then the Ministry of Information had issued a directive to editors that the normal rules for indicating the location of air raids on Southern England – identifying the Home Counties, London, etc – were suspended because 'it is particularly important to deny the enemy any information about the accuracy of his new weapons'. Only the general term 'Southern England' would henceforth be allowed in reports about raids and alerts. The Government had already issued guidelines to the Civil Defence about reporting 'crashed aircraft' that exploded on impact like the Kivik incident. So the Sarisbury Green claim remains a mystery that will probably never be answered.

There is no mystery about what happened in the early hours of Tuesday, 13 June 1944, a date that marks the beginning of the flying-bomb war. As the day dawned, four V-1s fell on England, the first at Swanscombe near Gravesend at 4.13am. Seven minutes later, Cuckfield in Sussex, 34 miles (54.7km) south of London, was hit. At 4.25am, the capital itself felt its first 'buzz bomb' (the name coming from the sound of the engine before it cut out and the rocket fell to earth), which fell on Grove Road in Bow, killing six people, injuring thirty and destroying the railway bridge that carried the Great Eastern Railway from Liverpool Street to Essex. Two hundred people were made homeless. Finally, at 5.06am, a fourth exploded at the Kent village of Platt, 5 miles (8km) north-east of Sevenoaks. There was no mention of any of this in British newspapers, and a briefing from the Ministry of Home Security declared that 'during darkness there was nothing to report'. That was true: daylight had broken when the first V-1s fell.

Five days later, on the morning of Sunday, 18 June, the Royal Military Chapel, popularly known as the Guards Chapel, at Wellington Barracks in Westminster was hit by a V-1. The chapel had been damaged by enemy action on several previous occasions, most notably during the Blitz in 1940 when its roof was set alight by incendiary bombs. This time, however, the strike proved devastating. The roof collapsed, killing 121 members of the congregation, both military and civilian, and injuring 141 others. With the exception of the apse, the chapel was completely destroyed, although six silver candlesticks survived, the candles in them still burning.

Britain's newspapers were concentrating on the pasting that the RAF had given the enemy that month. The *Birmingham Mail* reported that almost 4,000 tons (4,064 tonnes) of bombs had been dropped on targets in Germany and France. The *Daily Record* told how 'MPs and Peers crowded into the Grand Committee Room yesterday to watch a secret film entitled *The RAF in Combined Operations*. They saw RAF operational photographs and inspected a full-sized model of a 12,000lb bomb'.

But, while the public focus was on what the Allies were doing to German cities, at home Operation Diver, originally prepared in 1943, following the first reports of the 'revenge weapons', was implemented. A mixture of anti-aircraft guns, barrage balloons and fighter aircraft would soon be deployed against the V-1s and V-2s. A Royal New Zealand Air Force pilot, Arthur Umbers, described how he shot down a V-1 that was heading for Dover at about 3,000ft: 'One moment it was a "doodlebug" and the next it was a colossal mass of orange flame and black smoke.' Credited with shooting down at least fifteen flying bombs, 25-year-old Squadron Leader Arthur Umbers, DFC and Bar, lost his life over Germany on 14 February 1945. He is buried in Munster Heath War Cemetery.

In July 1944, Florence Horsbrugh, the Conservative MP for Dundee, and Parliamentary Secretary to the Ministry of Health, told the House of Commons that plans to evacuate tens of thousands of mothers and children had been made the previous September. Timetables had been set up, trains, mobilisation and reception points had all been arranged to deal with up to 10,000 people a day. 'In these difficult times we merely had to say, "Go ahead," and the machine worked,' she said to cheers from the House.

In the same debate, Captain Alec Cunningham-Reid, the Conservative member for St Marylebone, who had been awarded the DFC during service with the Royal Flying Corps in the First World War, wondered why 'we have not constructed flying bombs … Early in the war, the man who invented tanks, Major W.G. Wilson, invented a jet-propelled flying bomb simpler than the German one but with a bombing accuracy never heard of before'. He claimed that 'the Government put every obstacle in the way of developing this robot invention with the result that we have been caught napping'. Cunningham-Reid was a colourful character. In July 1943, in the lobby of the House of Commons, he had fought with fellow Tory MP Oliver Locker-Lampson (winner of the DSO while with the Royal Naval Air Service during the First World War), who had accused him of leaving London during the Blitz. It made news all over the world, the *Los Angeles Times* headlining the story, 'England grins as members of Commons trade punches'.

There were so many stories to come out of the V-1 and V-2 attacks. L.J. Goodey, of Loughton in Essex, recounted,

'Towards the end of 1944, the doodlebugs began their blitz on London. One day we were enjoying a swim in the River Roding, boys and girls together, all in the nude – the so-called pre-permissive days – when someone shouted, "Look up! It's coming straight for us!" We all jumped out of the water, grabbed what clobber we could and made for one of the trenches that they had dug in the fields to stop Jerry from landing. We had about 400yd [365m] to run and, in our panic, it seemed to follow us. We all sat shivering in the trench, waiting for it to cut out. Luckily, when it did, it crashed in Epping Forest.'

Many people regarded the attacks with typical British phlegm. In July 1944, at Lord's, a cricket match between the Army and the Royal Air Force was stopped when a V-1 was heard approaching the ground. The players lay on the turf, and spectators disappeared under the stands. But the rocket flew over the ground and landed in Regent's Park. Middlesex and England opening batsman Jack Robertson dusted himself down and celebrated the narrow escape by hitting the next ball for six. An outraged *Wisden Cricketers' Almanack*, the cricketer's 'Bible', later reported that this was 'the first flying-bomb to menace Lord's during the progress of a match'.

Etta Stern of Surbiton remembered,

'I was working in London, in Cannon Street, at the time of the doodlebugs – the flying bombs that came over, then cut out, and fell to earth. It was nerve-wracking. Once that engine stopped, you just waited for the explosion. One lunchtime, people were streaming out of their offices when we heard one coming over, so we just dived on to the pavement – which was muddy as it had been pouring with rain – and then there was silence, followed by this almighty bang a couple of streets away. We all got up and started off again when overcame another. Same thing – dive on the pavement, silence, big explosion. As I was getting up yet again, a little chap in front of me, wearing a cap, was also climbing to his feet. He looked at me and said: "Gettin' kinda 'umdrum, ain't it?"'

George Foster remembered, 'It would be late in 1944 and I was in a long queue, waiting for a bus. Suddenly we heard a doodlebug. Then all went quiet, and everyone chucked themselves on the floor. We had no idea where it was going to land. Fortunately, for us at least, it was some streets away. Everyone got back up and the queue reformed. Then I felt a tap on my shoulder. I turned around to see a "city gent". He said: "Excuse me, but I think I was in front of you." I won't tell you what I said to him.'

Wendy Holliman of Oxhey, Watford, recalled, 'I was sitting by the side of a lake at Rickmansworth, enjoying a peaceful afternoon, when I spotted an aircraft in the distance, and commented to my mother that the plane looked as though it was on fire! She lazily looked up from her book, realised it was a doodlebug – a V-1 rocket – grabbed my hand, and we ran along the lakeside to the tent where we were camping. The doodlebug dropped in Mill End, Rickmansworth, and the tent sides "whoofed" in and out with the blast. My mother suddenly started laughing and I couldn't understand why until she finally stopped, said: "How stupid, as if sheltering in a tent would give us any protection if the thing had dropped any nearer!"'

May Simpson, from Romford, who worked on an ARP mobile canteen throughout the Blitz, recalled, 'Hitler had just begun his doodlebug attacks, sending waves of the first of his secret weapons. They caused such widespread damage that communications were getting very strained, and the ambulance and rescue squads were getting adept at judging just where the fall would be after the V-1 engine cut out. One night a baby just three days old had been injured and was in hospital. Its mum was unharmed in the rest centre, and every three hours we would be collecting her to feed her baby. It was 5am. The milk round had started.'

In 1943, the People's Dispensary for Sick Animals had created the Allied Forces Mascot Club in order to recognise animals and birds that were serving the Allies during the war. A cat called Andrew became the club's mascot. Andrew did not himself go to war, but – stationed in London – he had to endure air raids on the capital, although it was reported that he kept calm and carried on sleeping through most of them. But he also seemed to know when a V-1 rocket attack was due and when Andrew took cover, everyone else knew that it was time to do so. Weighing more than 13lbs (6kg), he was a fawn-and-brown tabby with spotless white front, tummy and 'socks'. But, best of all, he boasted an inverted 'V for victory' on his nose. Winston Churchill no doubt approved of Andrew.

In August 1944, five London schoolboys, the eldest 13 and the youngest 11, evacuated to Exmouth the previous month, set out with the intention of walking back to the capital. Police found them near Crewkerne in Somerset, about 40 miles (64km) from Exmouth. The boys had spent two days and nights on the road, living on food given them by American soldiers, and apples from orchards. The constable who found them said that they told him that they wanted to get home to their mothers because they were worried about the doodlebugs.

On 7 September 1944, Duncan Sandys, chairman of the Cabinet Committee on Flying Bomb Counter-Measures, announced, 'Except for a few parting shots, what is going to be known as the Battle of London against the flying bomb is over.' The *Newcastle Journal*'s 'London Letter' columnist told how 'Londoners went to work today in cheerful mood … and they went home in crowded trains and buses tonight in even more cheerful mood – they had read the full thrilling story of how Southern England had won the Battle of the Flying Bombs'. Their optimism was premature. The next day, Hitler revealed an even more powerful revenge weapon, the V-2. What was effectively the world's first long-range guided ballistic missile fell first on Chiswick in West London, causing multiple casualties. The 46ft (14m) long rocket was powered by a liquid propellant engine and flew at supersonic speed. It was the work of Wernher von Braun, a German rocket engineer who would later play a pivotal role in the US Moon landings. He developed the V-2 at Peenemünde Army Research Centre on the island of Usedom in the Baltic Sea. Like the V-1, it had been built at the cost of thousands of lives of slave labourers. Following a devasting raid by the RAF on Peenemünde in August 1943, the German High Command had moved missile assembly to underground sites, the main one at a former gypsum mine close to Nordhausen in Thuringia, on the border of the southern Harz Mountains. Here a concentration camp was established – Mittelbau-Dora, a sub-camp of Buchenwald – and its inmates were forced to excavate nearby mineshafts. From January 1944, V-1 and V-2 rockets were assembled here. The workers' conditions were inhumane and around one in three of the 60,000 sent to Mittelbau-Dora died there.

Some 1,000 V-2s were aimed at Britain, causing an estimated 2,700 deaths. At 12.26pm on Saturday, 25 November 1944, a V-2 made a direct hit on a crowded Woolworth's store in London's New Cross. One hundred and sixty-eight people were killed outright, some of them in a neighbouring Co-op shop. The victims included thirty-three children, including babies in their prams. One hundred and twenty-three passers-by were also injured, many seriously. It was a scene of absolute carnage, blood, shattered glass, overturned vehicles. *The People* reported,

'Shoppers crowded the pavements of a main road in Southern England during one of the week's busiest periods recently when a V-bomb fell. Women and children were buried beneath the burning wreckage of two buildings. Amid a grim scene, searchlights helped in the search for trapped victims. Several passengers in a passing bus were killed. Beneath a car, at the wheel of which the driver was found dead, were the bodies of other people blown there by the blast. In another V-bomb incident, doctors and rescuers climbed precariously among tottering and crumbling masonry to reach trapped victims in a luncheon club.'

The very nature of the V-rockets was that they did not discriminate, and the royal family were in as much danger as anyone else. Like millions of other youngsters, the royal princesses, Elizabeth and Margaret Rose, spent much of the war in the relative safety of the British countryside, although in their case it was at Windsor Castle, which was close enough to London that residents would often spend nights sleeping in the cellars in case of overnight air raids.

Hitler had apparently fancied retaining the iconic royal residence as his own following a Nazi invasion, and the castle itself did not receive any direct hits. However, the town itself was bombed on a number of occasions and the worst attack came in the form of V-1s, on the first day of July 1944. Marion Crawford had been employed by the king and queen as governess to their daughters and, according to her unauthorised account published upon her retirement, she had been with the princesses in Windsor Great Park that morning. The group had been cooking sausages with the Girl Guides when they caught sight of a doodlebug approaching the park. 'Crawfie', as she was known to the princesses, instructed the party to lie on the ground. The governess threw herself protectively over Margaret, and the terrified group waited until the rocket flew on before crashing on to Windsor racecourse. Another V-1 hit the town's 'dust destructor' waste incineration plant, sending shards of glass flying and injuring sixty people.

Britain was not the only target of Hitler's revenge weapons. Belgium suffered too. At 3.20pm on 16 December 1944 – the first day of the Battle of the Bulge – a V-2 fell on the liberated city of Antwerp. It scored a direct hit on the Rex cinema in Avenue De Keyserle where a sell-out audience was watching *The Plainsman*, a film about Buffalo Bill, when there was a flash of light, a deafening explosion, and the balcony and ceiling came crashing down. It was the bloodiest day in the history of flying bombs. A total of 537 people were killed, including 296 British, US and Canadian soldiers; 291 people were injured and 11 buildings were destroyed. Many of the dead were removed to Antwerp's zoo where they were laid out for identification, and it took the authorities more than a week to clear the site. It was the biggest death toll from a single rocket attack during the war in Europe.

By the spring of 1945, the reign of terror wrought by the revenge weapons was over as Allied troops overran the launch sites. The last V-2 to land on British soil did so on 27 March 1945, killing one person in Orpington, Kent. Earlier that same day, however, 134 men, women and children, many of them Jews, died when a V-2 hit Hughes Mansions in Vallance Road, Stepney. The death toll was exceeded only by the New Cross tragedy of the previous November.

According to the National Archives, 6,725 V-1s were launched at Britain. Of these, 2,340 hit London, causing 5,475 deaths, with 16,000 injured. The final V-1 crashed in Datchworth in Hertfordshire, 30 miles (48km) north of London on 29 March 1945. It was an inglorious end to Hitler's much vaunted revenge weapon campaign: the rocket fell in a field close to a sewage farm at Woolmer Green, at 9am. There were no casualties.

Chapter 11

Service Without Thought of Reward

*At last I can say that you have fulfilled your charge. The Home Guard has
reached the end of its long tour of duty under arms.*

King George VI

O n 4 September 1944, Britain's Home Guard units received a letter
from the War Office: 'During the past months the Home Guard
has performed a vital service by enabling the regular forces to leave
this country, by providing protection against the danger of potential enemy
interference. This danger has not yet disappeared.

'The Home Guard has also given the most valuable service in assisting the
civil defence organisations and the public in connection with the attacks
by flying missiles. This danger also has not yet passed. It is therefore
necessary that the Home Guard should continue to take the place of
the regular forces until, in the opinion of His Majesty's Government, all
dangers are past.

'The success of the campaign on the Continent points to the likelihood
of this date being near, and it is necessary to have the machinery ready
for the standing down of the Home Guard in order that the detail can
be worked out and thus result in a smooth and quick operation when the
time comes.'

It was on 14 May 1940 that the Secretary of State for War, Anthony Eden,
had asked for volunteers, aged between 17 and 65, for what would be called the
Local Defence Volunteer Force. In August, the new Prime Minister, Winston
Churchill, ordered the name to be changed to the Home Guard. What would
become a legend in British history was born.

The original idea was that this citizens' army would try to delay invading
German forces until the regular army could be rushed to the scene. But they
were poorly armed and, as brave as they might have been, it was difficult to
imagine them, using only a collection of sporting and museum-piece firearms
and bread knives tied to broom handles, holding back a highly trained, well-
armed force. Eventually, better arms and better training transformed the

original rag-tag army into an organisation that may well have proved an inconvenience to German paratroopers.

The forming of the Home Guard was a response to what was already happening. As the threat of invasion became very real, up and down the country there were reports of bands of civilians arming themselves with shotguns, air-rifles and pitchforks, ready to stick it to the Hun. The Government had two options: to quash these grass-roots resistance fighters; or to harness them into an official organisation. Thus, the Local Defence Volunteers were formed without any budget or any staff. And from there, as the Home Guard, it developed into something resembling a military force.

The early signs were encouraging, at least from the point of view of numbers if not of efficiency. Eden had told those interested to register their names at their local police station and they would be contacted when required. Inside the first 24 hours, more than a quarter of a million men had left their details, more than had been in Britain's regular peacetime army.

The Government anticipated that around 150,000 men might answer the call to part-time arms. By the end of the second month, over one million had applied to join the LDV ('Look, Duck and Vanish' as it was unkindly dubbed in some quarters). By the time of that War Office notice four years later, although the threat of invasion had long since passed, its number stood at 1.7 million. At that point, the Home Guard had lost more than 1,200 members who were killed during air raids or died later from injuries they had received.

The relationship between the Home Guard and the War Office was generally an uneasy one. Lieutenant General Sir Henry Royds Pownall, the first Inspector General of the Local Defence Volunteer Force, complained: 'They are a troublesome and querulous lot … there is mighty little pleasing them, and the minority is always noisy.' (In the interests of balance, it should be noted that historian Brian D. Osborne, in his account of the Home Guard in Scotland, wrote that although Lieutenant General Pownall – who was Chief of General Staff for the British Expeditionary Force in France and Belgium until the fall of France in May 1940 – might have appeared 'a high quality appointment', in fact Field Marshal Montgomery thought him 'completely useless').

There were plenty of people who regarded the Home Guard in a similar light. Shortly after the announcement was made that it would be stood down, someone signing themselves 'Common Sense' wrote to the *Rochdale Observer* in response to another announcement that Civil Defence duties were to be relaxed: 'It is the writer's opinion that the Regional Commissioners will oppose any relaxation as so many cushy jobs would "go west". The Home Guard could also do with cutting down, and, in fact, works companies could be abolished, as, for a long time, they have been seen as a standing joke.'

There were many stories. George Watson, who in September 1944, as an RAF squadron leader, located, in a Norwegian fjord, the German battleship *Tirpitz* that threatened Allied shipping, recalled, 'I was flying a Miles Magister over Allestree Park in Derby. Our brief was to give the Home Guard a chance to guess at what height we were flying and let them have a bit of aiming practice as well. Only when we got back to base did we realise they were using live ammunition. One bullet had gone straight between my knees. The young officer in charge told an inquiry: "We thought they were armour-plated. In any case, we never thought we'd hit them!"'

Others, however, especially those in charge of the Home Guard, were dismayed at the news of an impending stand down. Lieutenant Colonel Thomas Washington-Metcalfe, who commanded the 11th Somerset (Ilminster) Battalion, said that the decision was 'very much to be regretted'.

'The announcement regarding the suspension of compulsory parades was made in such a manner, hastily following a campaign by certain newspapers as to give the impression that the Home Guard was to be allowed to fade out from Monday, 11 September – disappear by slow decline and be buried obscurely instead of passing out with the recognition and ceremony it so richly deserves … I hope that when the time comes our disembodiment will be with public honours.'

On that account, Lieutenant Colonel Washington-Metcalfe need not have been concerned. There would certainly be parades to mark the moment.

Meanwhile, on 8 September 1944, the political correspondent of the *Daily News* wondered, 'Must the Home Guard give up his boots?'

'Sir James Grigg, the War Minister, stated in his Wednesday night broadcast that even voluntary duties might be discontinued before the war with Germany ends … the removal of compulsory duties from Monday next was announced by Sir James as "a very willing payment on account". Home Guards would welcome a final payment in the form of an order that those who desire should be allowed to keep their uniforms, greatcoats, and, particularly, their army boots. At the moment there is doubt whether they will be able to keep little more than their cap badge. In four years Home Guards have worn out millions of pairs of socks for which they had to forfeit coupons. The amateur gardeners, the allotment holders, the road labourers and the workers in heavy industry will expect at least to keep their boots, khaki trousers and possibly greatcoats coupon-free for private use.'

Again, there would be no need to worry on that score.

On the same day, General Sir Frederick Pile, commander-in-chief of Anti-Aircraft Command, had a message to Home Guard units manning AA batteries:

'In certain parts of the country, air attack is most unlikely, and in these parts I suggest that, from time to time, you should visit your old batteries, just to keep your hands in. There are, however, a few areas at which Hitler may still have a crack. Obviously London is the principal target.' Sir Frederick asked Home Guards in the capital and other still vulnerable areas to support the regular gunners for the next fortnight. 'At the end of that,' he said, 'I think our homes should be safe and, if so, we will ask you to come occasionally and see us.'

On 20 September, Major A.E. Hickman, adjutant of Birmingham's Home Guard, in which almost 60,000 men served, said that there was still no news about when they would be stood down:

'We have heard nothing at all. Plans are in place but, in the absence of any definite instructions, we are "standing easy". In the meantime, training is being continued for those men who desire it – and there are quite a number of them – and it takes the form of training parades every other Sunday. A certain number of men are also willing to carry out picket duties at headquarters, where the arms, ammunition and documents are kept, until we are authorised what to do. Uniforms are supposed to be withdrawn with the stand down order, but representations have been made throughout the country to retain the uniforms at least until the victory parades are over. But the answer to that I cannot tell you.'

Eventually, the news came: the Home Guard would be stood down from Wednesday, 1 November 1944. The *Daily Herald* reported,

'The Home Guard will be on the reserve, but still liable for emergency duties, from the day after tomorrow. That is the official date for the stand down. It is emphasised that the corps is not yet to be disbanded. Stand down parades are to be held all over the country on Sunday, 3 December, when the King, as Colonel-in-Chief, will broadcast a message of appreciation and thanks … The King has approved the grant of honorary rank to all Home Guard officers. Every NCO and man is to receive a certificate of service signed by the King. The War Office announcement said: "The stand down, which entails the concentration of weapons and other equipment, will take some time to complete, and Home Guard units will be occupied with this task for the next two months." And so in effect the Home Guard, four and a half years old, virtually ceases to exist after its final parade on 3 December.'

At 3pm on that first Sunday in December, more than 7,000 men – some very young, some very old – began their march through a leafless Hyde Park, where they saluted their Colonel-in-Chief, King George VI. They came from all parts of Britain, men from the Orkneys and the Highlands, from the West Country and Wales, from the Midlands and East Anglia, from the Home Counties, from hundreds of cities, towns and villages throughout Britain. Excluding officers there were meant to be three men from each unit in Britain. The balance was made up from London District.

The king, in the uniform of a field marshal, with the queen dressed in black, and Princesses Elizabeth and Margaret Rose in grey, stood on a dais at Stanhope Gate taking the farewell salute. With the king on the saluting base were the War Minister, Sir James Grigg, and the Commander-in-Chief of the Home Forces, General Sir Harold Franklin. Below them were three field marshals – Sir Claud Jacob, Lord Milne and Lord Craven – and Lieutenant General Sir Keith Anderson of Eastern Command; Major General James Drew, the Director General of the Home Guard; Sir Harold Howitt of the Air Council; Lord Croft, the Under-Secretary of State for War; Albert Alexander, the First Lord of the Admiralty.

The band of the Irish Guards played opposite the dais, and for forty-two minutes the Home Guard marched past, six abreast, then on to Piccadilly, Piccadilly Circus, Oxford Street, Marble Arch, Tyburn Gate, through Hyde Park again, and then towards their dispersal point at the Ring Road.

That evening, at 9pm, on the BBC, the king broadcast the nation's 'Thank you'.

'Most of you have been engaged for long hours in work necessary for the prosecution of the war, or to maintaining the healthful life of the nation, and you have given a great portion of the time which should have been your own to learn the skilled work of a soldier. By this patient, ungrudging effort, you have built and maintained a force able to play an essential part in the defence of our threatened soil and liberty. I have long wished to see you relieved of this burden, but it would have been a betrayal of all we owe to our fathers and our sons if any step had been taken which might have imperilled our country's safety. At last I can say that you have fulfilled your charge … You have gained something for yourselves. You have discovered in yourselves new capabilities. You have found how men from all kinds of homes and many different occupations can work together in a great cause, and how happy they can be with each other. For most of you – and I must add for your wives – your service in the Home Guard has not been easy. I know what it has meant, especially for older men. I am very proud of what the Home Guard has done, and I give my heartfelt thanks to all. Officers, non-commissioned officers and men, you have served your country with a steadfast devotion. I know that your country will not forget that service.'

The King had made many visits with Home Guard units throughout the war, and the Home Guard had taken its turn in mounting the guard at Buckingham Palace.

The following day, the *Daily Mirror* added its thanks: 'The folk of all Britain, cheered and said, "Well done!" as the Home Guard marched through the capital yesterday.' It was not just in London that the Home Guard marched, however.

In Bristol, each battalion first paraded in its own area before converging on the city for a ceremonial march-past along a route lined ten deep by thousands of people. In Hull, 2,000 Home Guards marched to Corporation Field to the strains of *Keep The Home Fires Burning* and *Where Are The Boys Of The Old Brigade?* played by regimental bands.

The Goole companies of the West Riding Home Guard, some 350 strong, marched to the parish church for the standing down service, and Bridlington's Priory Church was filled as the 5th East Riding Battalion was stood down. In Rochdale, mist and heavy drizzle greeted 500 men of the Rochdale Battalion when they formed up in the Town Hall Square to hear their commanding officer, Lieutenant Colonel E.A. Stringer MC, read the King's Special Army Order, part of which read, 'History will say that your share in the greatest of all our struggles for freedom was a vitally important one. You have given your service without thought of reward.'

The weather spoiled many parades. The *Derby Evening Telegraph* reported,

'Derby's Home Guard marched out of the war picture with mud-caked boots and rain-sodden. It was a fitting finale. Those three hours of standing or striding in the downpour – real "Home Guard weather" – that saluted their stand down ceremony in Markeaton Park were uncomfortably illustrative of their hard going during the past four years while Britain weathered her worst storm.'

One year later, on 31 December 1945, the *Daily Herald* headline reported, 'The HG dies at 2400 hrs':

'From midnight tonight, the Home Guard will be only a memory. The world's greatest civilian army will be disbanded, and its 1,700,000 members will be free to do what they like with the equipment that has not been called in. Khaki greatcoats can be converted to civilian use. Any tailor who has the time will get them dyed for you for £2. For a few more shillings he will remove the brass buttons – it is illegal to wear them – and sew on civilian ones. The result – a half-belt overcoat without coupons. The old battledress can be used in the garden or for work. Just see that flashes and badges of rank are removed. No fanfares of trumpets will salute the passing of the Home Guard. That was all done when it stood down in September.'

There were a few modest ceremonies, however. In Devon, Major J.G. Bentley, officer commanding 'F' Company Paignton, made a personal gift to each of his officers – 'a petrol lighter of special make and design with the Home Guard crest on the cover'. Each was engraved with the initials of the recipient. In West Cornwell, the Porthleven Detachment of 'A' Company, 8th Battalion Home Guard, held a stand down musical evening in the town's Public Hall. There was community singing and a concert. A vote of thanks was accorded to Mr F. Bartle, who, although considerably over age, was one of the original LDV members, and was quartermaster sergeant for over three years without missing a parade. Wives of members served refreshments.

In Hull, former members of 8th South Riding Battalion, Home Guard, were invited to a meeting at Wenlock Barracks in Anlaby Road to discuss the forming of an old comrades' association. In South Shields, members of a Royal Artillery anti-aircraft battery advertised their own pantomime, *Babes in the Wood*, to be put on at the town's drill hall. Most of the cast belonged to the Royal Artillery unit that had been responsible for training the 101st (Durham) Home Guard Anti-aircraft Rocket Battery, which had consisted of men from South Shields, Jarrow, Hebburn and Gateshead. It was hoped that many of the Home Guards and their relatives and friends would support the pantomime. There would be no charge for admission, but a collection would be taken for the prisoners of war fund.

The Home Guard was no more, but the camaraderie and the tales lived on for decades after the war. If the Nazis had invaded the British mainland, even if their effectiveness would have been minimal, who is to say that the real Dad's Army wouldn't have fought bravely? In the meantime, they kept calm and carried on.

Chapter 12

The Day The World Exploded

This sixth year of war has been noteworthy for by far the biggest explosion ever to have occurred in these islands.

HM Inspector of Explosives report

The morning newspapers on Monday, 27 November 1944 were full of the usual war news. Two thousand fighter-bombers backed up the Allied armies as the Aachen front flared up into a new ferocity. The RAF was again making pinpoint attacks on V-2 rocket sites in Holland. Reports were just filtering through of a V-2 attack in 'Southern England' that weekend, that had claimed the lives of 'numerous Christmas shoppers'. Major David Currie of the Canadian Armoured Corps had been awarded the Victoria Cross for 'scouting, tank-killing and directing a battle for three days with only an hour's sleep', which had slashed the escape route of 3,000 German troops in the Falaise Gap three months earlier. And, in Burma, British troops had taken the village of Nanbon from the Japanese.

At home, the problem of dockside thieving was growing as parcels of comforts – cigarettes, tobacco, chocolate etc – destined for troops serving overseas were being pilfered in ever increasing numbers. West Ham Town Council called for the appointment of a Minister with Cabinet rank to deal with the problem of war-damaged houses and rehousing in general. And the wholesale price of Christmas trees was going up to about 1s 6d (8p) a foot because no trees were being imported this year.

There was one other news item that caught the eye:

'Three miners entombed by a fall of roof at Measham Main Colliery near Burton upon Trent on Saturday were found dead when rescue parties reached them after twenty-eight hours' ceaseless work. A gang was clearing a heavy fall of roof when a further fall of hundreds of tons engulf them … relatives of the three men waited at the pithead, but very little hope was held out for them as no tappings could be heard. Rescue work continued without pause until the bodies were found. Two others caught by the fall were saved.'

The tragedy would have no doubt been on the minds of the men turning up for work that Monday at RAF Fauld, an underground munitions storage depot just to the east of the Staffordshire village of Hanbury. In 1937, as the prospect of another war with Germany loomed even more, the Air Ministry had purchased 450,000sq ft (4,180sq m) of disused gypsum mine workings at Fauld for weapons storage. It was seen as a good place to store explosives, 90ft (27m) underground, in a rural location, and where mining had left natural rock pillars to support the roof. The RAF added a concrete roof and two concrete walls, one of them 50ft (15m) thick, to separate explosives from incendiaries. By November 1944, around 500 servicemen and 450 civilians working there were joined by 195 Italian prisoners of war brought from a POW camp at nearby Hilton. Bombs were stored in bunkers along 18,000sq ft (1,672sq m) of the concrete-lined corridors at what was RAF Maintenance Unit 21. A narrow-gauge railway was used to pull wagons loaded with bombs out of store.

At 11.11am on 27 November, Joseph West, who farmed at Cubley, 8 miles (12.8km) from Fauld, heard an explosion. A little while later, a neighbour told him that there had been an accident at the RAF store. His brothers, Stephen and John, were working at Upper Castle Hayes Farm, which sat on top of the disused mine. He set off to find them. But there was no sign of them. In fact, there was no trace of Upper Castle Hayes Farm. It had disappeared in one of the largest non-nuclear explosions in the history of mankind.

Wartime censorship meant that only the barest details were published at the time, about an accident in which some seventy people died, an untold number of others were injured and there was huge damage to property over a wide area.

Seismologists in Morocco and in Switzerland recorded the blast as between 3,500 to 4,000 tons (3,556 to 4,064 tonnes) as ordnance, from high-explosive bombs to shells and rifle ammunition, exploded. Almost every house in the village of Hanbury was badly damaged, the Cock Inn there lost half its roof and Upper Castle Hayes Farm vanished completely. Two church steeples in Burton upon Trent, more than 3 miles (5km) away, were cracked, and houses there suffered blast damage. A pupil at Burton Grammar School later recalled how a physics laboratory there 'swayed from side to side'. There were reports of the explosion being heard at Daventry, 19 miles (30km) south of Coventry, and at Weston-Super-Mare, more than 130 miles (20km) from Fauld.

Rescue work took more than three months and was hampered by pockets of gas, 6 million gallons (27,276,540 litres) of water from a nearby reservoir and 10,000 tons (10,160 tonnes) of rubble. The US Army with its earth-moving equipment was early on hand but it was a gargantuan job.

Debris had risen out of sight into the sky before falling back for more than three hours, covering a huge area in four inches of dust. The blast left

Allied troops preparing to land in Normandy, D-Day, 6 June 1944. (*Illustrated London News*)

General Bernard Montgomery, Commander of overall Allied ground operations on D-Day. (*Illustrated London News*)

Hermann Goreing asked if he should assume leadership of the Third Reich in the event that Hitler was unable to govern. (*Illustrated London News*)

Herman Goreing (second from left) shows Martin Bormann (at left) damage in Hitler's HQ after the assassination attempt of 20 July 1944. (*Alamy*)

The aftermath of the first V-2 missile to fall on the UK, on Staveley Road, Chiswick, West London on 8 September 1944. (*Alamy*)

Mothers and their children evacuated from London to the Midlands to escape the flying bombs in September 1944. (*Authors' collection*)

Captured British paratroopers at Arnhem, September 1944. (*Alamy*)

Tanks and infantrymen of the 82nd Airborne Division push through the snow in Belgium during the Battle of the Bulge in December 1944. (*Alamy*)

The ruins of Dresden in February 1945, looking south from the Rathaus, past the August Schreitmueller sculpture 'Güte' ('kindness'). (*Alamy*)

The 'Big Three', Winston Churchill, Franklin D. Roosevelt and Joseph Stalin, at Yalta in February 1945. (*Illustrated London News*)

Adolf Hitler, in typical pose. By April 1945, though, he was a broken man. (*Illustrated London News*)

Winston Churchill sitting in a broken chair outside Hitler's former bunker in Berlin, July 1945. (*Alamy*)

Charles de Gaulle, the leader of the Free French forces. (*Illustrated London News*)

Heinrich Himmler, architect of the Holocaust, committed suicide on 23 May 1945, after being captured by Russians and handed over to British forces. (*Illustrated London News*)

Happy scenes in London's Fleet Street on VE Day. (*Alamy*)

One of the hundreds of street parties that celebrated VE Day, 8 May 1945. (*Alamy*)

A Midlands street decked out to celebrate the end of the war in Europe. (*Authors' collection*)

a crater 100ft (30m) deep and, at its widest, 1,007ft (307m) across. Besides the complete destruction of Upper Castle Hayes Farm, Hanbury Fields Farm, Hare Holes Farm and Croft Farm and its adjoining cottages were also extensively damaged. The biggest single loss of life – thirty-one killed – was at the Peter Ford & Sons' plaster works, which was destroyed when the dam wall of the reservoir was breached, sending a mudslide carrying earth and rocks down on to the works and drowning and burying workers.

There were many stories including that of the elderly couple who, four hours after the blast, were found in their farmhouse still staring at each other, debris from their roof mixed with the meal that they had been eating. And the dead cow, inflated to twice its normal size by air pressure, still standing on the spot where it had died. It was one of 200 cattle that perished that day. Fields were littered with dead livestock and fish. It was as if a plague of biblical proportion had descended on this hitherto sleepy part of Staffordshire.

There were also many instances of bravery that day, and in the days that followed. Dr Godfrey Rotter, an Air Ministry scientific adviser, and Eric Bryant, 21 MU's resident engineer, together with Joseph Salt, a foreman in charge of civilian staff at the mine, were each awarded the George Medal for gallantry in clearing the mine in the aftermath of the explosion. Dr Rotter was responsible for evacuating the explosive stores:

'Dr Rotter's example was outstanding. … he displayed courage of a very high order.' Eric Bryant was the first to enter the damaged parts of the mine, his work requiring him to climb over rock falls overlying explosives in a dangerous state. Joseph Salt's commendation read, 'He was much shaken but remained in the mine until everyone in his area had been evacuated. On reaching the mine entrance he gave considerable assistance in removing casualties. He then re-entered the mine, found an injured man and carried him out. The foreman again went underground, this time with an oxygen mask, as a member of a rescue party. In the course of an extensive search of the damaged area, four of this party had to retire because of the effects of fumes. Later he entered the mine for a third time to act as guide to rescue teams. Eventually, he had to be assisted into the open suffering from the effects of fumes. Foreman Salt showed great courage and was indefatigable in his efforts.'

Sidney Maxted, a scientific adviser to the Ministry of Supply, was awarded the OBE, and George Fox, an RAF leading storeman, Ernest Parker, a machine operator, and Horace Utting, a quarryman, were each awarded the British Empire Medal (Civil Division). They were among more than twenty men, including members of the North Warwickshire Mines Rescue Station at Wilnecote, who were commended for their bravery in entering fume-filled tunnels, looking for survivors.

After the explosion, the local coroner, John Auden, conducted an inquest into sixty-eight victims (which included six Italian prisoners of war), nineteen of whose bodies had not been found. The Home Office had given permission to include in the inquest findings the bodies presumed to be irrecoverable. The final death toll is uncertain but is generally thought to be seventy-two. Almost three years later, in August 1947, Mr Auden reopened an inquest on one of the missing. Workmen operating a bulldozer had uncovered the remains of Stephen West, the tractor driver who had been working at Upper Castle Hayes Farm at Hanbury. Mr Auden could now notify the Home Secretary to delete Stephen West's name from the list of bodies not recovered.

Joseph West told the inquest that he had seen his brother on the evening of the day before the explosion. He identified two tobacco pipes, a tobacco pouch, a belt from a waterproof coat and a leather belt as belonging to Stephen. The discovery was made about 200yd (183m) from the edge of the main crater where the body of the other brother, John, had been found ten days after the explosion.

Mr Auden paid tribute to the work of four inmates of Stafford prison, who had helped police to recover Stephen West's remains from heavy clay. Their efforts were worthy of commendation, and the coroner said that he would write to the prison governor to that effect. In October 1947, the men's sentences were each reduced by twenty-one days. The previous year, two 20-year-old prisoners from Stafford had escaped from a working party of 100 men who were restoring land devastated by the explosion at Fauld.

In January 1947, the 1944 claim by Joseph Goebbels that the Fauld explosion was caused by a V-2 rocket was refuted in the annual report of HM Inspector of Explosives. In 1974, it was announced that the likely cause was bombs being primed for use and replaced in storage with their detonators still installed. A worker claimed to have seen a colleague using a brass chisel, rather than the regulation wooden batten, to work on removing a faulty detonator from a live bomb.

On 1 December 1944, the Air Minister, Sir Archibald Sinclair, told the House of Commons that a court of inquiry had been ordered to investigate. 'The total loss of bombs is less than 4,000 tons, no more than has been dropped in a single raid on Germany ... I deeply regret that this disaster has been attended by severe loss of life and damage to private property.' Replying to John Gretton, the Conservative MP for Burton, Sir Archibald, said that if the preliminary impression that the disaster was not due to enemy action was correct, then compensation to civilians would be the responsibility of his department. In the meantime, officials had been sent down to give help and payments to those who had suffered and urgently required help. In due course, the Air Ministry agreed to pay damages totalling £41,686 to relatives of twenty-two members of the Transport and General Workers' Union who were killed in the blast. The awards ranged from more than £4,000 for a widow and six children, to £325 to a married daughter not dependent. A local relief fund totalled £7,831 by the end of December 1945. Today, there is little sign of the death and destruction. The crater left by the Fauld explosion is now filled with trees, and the paths around it are popular with walkers.

Chapter 13

Christmas Returns Again!

I'll Be Home For Christmas, You Can Count on Me ...
Walter Kent, Kim Gannon and Buck Ram,
recorded by Bing Crosby, December 1943

In August 1914, there was talk that the war might be 'over by Christmas'. In September 1939, there was no such illusion. Come the early autumn of 1944, however, even the most pessimistic Britons had begun to think that, after D-Day, it just might be so. Until mid-December, that was. When the Germans began their Ardennes Offensive and resumed their doodlebug attacks on England, it was clear that Hitler was not finished yet. In the early morning of Christmas Eve, an area across Northern England was peppered with more than thirty V-2 rockets. Although the attack was concentrated on what we now know as Greater Manchester, areas as far apart as Epworth in Lincolnshire, Spennymoor in County Durham and Newport in Shropshire were also hit.

Nevertheless, things were looking brighter. News of Allied advances was encouraging and, on the Home Front, the Ministry of Food had announced that there were to be special Christmas rations, with extra sugar, margarine and meat available. Vegetarians were to be permitted extra cheese, children could have extra sweets and the over-70s would receive extra tea. And for everyone there would be a quarter of a pound (142g) of nuts. To ensure that everyone could have their ration, shoppers were encouraged not to take more than their fair share of nuts. In reality, keeping supply up with demand for said nuts proved difficult for many shopkeepers, who soon grew tired of being asked for them.

Throughout the war, housewives had relied heavily upon the co-operation of the Ministry of Food to provide their festive feast. It distributed a colourful leaflet containing advice and plenty of seasonal recipes for items like Christmas pudding, which featured dried eggs, a nutmeg sauce and a Christmas cake that could be decorated with mock marzipan made from an unlikely combination of water, margarine, almond essence, sugar and soya flour. The cake could be given a thin icing, providing that households chose to take their sugar ration in its icing version. There was also something called 'Snow Pudding' – a concoction of sugar, semolina, apple pulp and milk – which was decorated with coloured sugar. There was little chance of a turkey, of course, but that was nothing new, although S.J. McDowell of Ballymena did declare itself 'open to receive your supplies of turkeys, geese, ducks and other fowl'.

At 1.15pm on Christmas Eve 1944, Colonel John Llewellin broadcast a festive message on the BBC. While settling down to listen to the radio was very much a key part of any Christmas celebration, a pep-talk from the Minister of Food probably was not one of the main draws. Much more appealing was the generally light-hearted programming offered by the two services available – the Home Service and the General Forces Programme. Music, fun and, it being Christmas, a smattering of religious programming kept families entertained from Christmas Eve through to Boxing Day. There were orchestras and dance bands, and a concert by the Brighouse and Rastrick brass band, as well as a Christmas special of the long-running *Kentucky Minstrels* – a blackface variety show. Comedian Will Hay entertained listeners, there was an episode of *In Town Tonight* and a 'narrated radio version' of the original musical comedy *Sunny*, starring Jack Buchanan and Elsie Randolph.

Just in case anyone was likely to forget that there was still 'a war on' there were also regular news bulletins. Christmas Day itself offered special children's programmes as well as an ENSA (the Entertainments National Service Association) show and, at 2pm, *The Journey Home*, which was described in the *Radio Times* thus: 'The peoples of the British Commonwealth and their Allies are linked again by radio to greet the men and women everywhere fighting in the cause of freedom, and to send special greetings to the families of Europe who are home again this Christmas Day.'

At 3pm the king made his final Christmas Day broadcast of the war. With his wife and daughters sitting beside him, his words touched upon the successes of the past year and broached the idea that the Allies would finally prevail. Already, he said, some of the lamps that the Germans had put out all over Europe were being rekindled and were beginning to shine through the fog of war.

'At this Christmas time we think proudly and gratefully of our fighting men wherever they may be. May God bless and protect them and bring them victory.' He sent his good wishes to the sick and wounded in hospitals and the medical staff caring for them; for prisoners of war and the relatives waiting at home for their return – 'Families rent apart by the call of service, people sundered from people by the calamities that have overwhelmed some' – and for those people of the Empire who had helped bring victory so near and whose aim was 'a world of free men, untouched by tyranny'.

The two princesses had kept themselves busy in the build-up to Christmas. For the previous three years, they had found a traditionally British way to help local children celebrate what had become subdued festive seasons. The Christmas of 1944 saw them present their fourth Royal Pantomime – entitled *Old Mother Red-Riding Boots* – and the three performances in Windsor Castle's Waterloo Chamber featured fifteen local schoolchildren, as well as some of their own friends. Money raised was donated to the Royal Household Wool Fund, which supplied yarns with which to knit comforts for the troops.

Of course, pantomimes were for everyone, not just royalty. Up and down the country, theatres filled with families keen to experience that festive silliness. In Liverpool, at the Empire Theatre, it was *Babes in the Wood*. The Babes were played by Ethel Revnell and Gracie West – a popular comedy duo whose act played on the notable differential in their heights – Revnell stood 6ft (1.8m) tall, West just 5ft (1.5m). In Derby, the cast of the Grand Theatre's production of *Humpty Dumpty* included Jimmy Clitheroe in the title role. He stood only 4ft 2ins (1.27m) and was familiar playing a perpetual schoolboy, despite celebrating his 23rd birthday during the run. The cast also included, according to the *Derby Evening Telegraph*, 'vivacious Margaret Morgan', who possessed a 'twinkling sense of humour, a pair of shapely legs and a grand mezzo-soprano voice'. A regular in the principal boy role, she explained how wartime shortages had affected her professionally: 'Fully-fashioned silk tights are essential for my part. Thank goodness I have a stock by me. They are impossible to get now. Even so, it's like asking for the Moon to get them dyed certain colours.' There were no such problems for Frank O'Brian, who was donning 'bonnet and wig, frills and furbelows'. A veteran of the First World War with the Durham Light Infantry, he told a reporter, 'I've been cast as the dame again. Never mind, it's the grandest fun in the world.'

It wasn't just Margaret Morgan who was struggling to find what she wanted in British shops. As the big day approached, manufacturers and businesses placed newspaper advertisements hoping to persuade customers that they had the answer to their Christmas present worries. Like Arding and Hobbs Ltd, a department store on the corner of Lavender Hill and St John's Road in Battersea. They could offer Musiflor perfume by Avy, 'a delightful fragrance', for 15s (75p); an elegant snakeskin zip powder compact, which came in a choice of tan, blue, green and maroon for 32s 6d (£1.53); artificial pearls for 29s 9d (£1.49); books for children at 6s (30p); embroidered linen handkerchiefs at 8s 10d (44p); and hanger sets with shoe trees of various colours in a cellophane packaging for 8s 2d (41p). Another local department store, Thurman and Malin of St Peter's Street, Derby – 'always an excellent choice' – boasted, 'The firm's buyers have been successful in securing an attractive selection of Useful Gifts and Novelties for the Christmas season.' McBride's of Bridge Street, Ballymena, offered a 'good assortment' of gifts for the more religiously minded with 'Bibles, Psalters and Church Hymnary, Prayer and Hymnals, Scripture and Motto Cards' as well as the usual books, novels and what it called 'the Irish Calendar'.

In Bristol, Taylor's of the Green, using its 'wartime home' on Whiteladies Road, offered life's finer things: 'fancy linens', cut glass and antique furniture. While, across the street, Jolly & Sons stocked the usual underwear, handkerchiefs, jumpers and so on. The store also drew attention to its Bath branch, which had a furniture department where ornamental rugs, old pewter and brass, and decorative china were on sale.

Amidst the advertisements for presents, and food and drink with which to fill the Christmas table, companies that manufactured items not currently available due to ration restrictions also sought to remind Britons of their popular products. 'Christmas returns again! … and soon, we hope, will Idris quality soft drinks', declared the manufacturers of its 'quality table waters through five successive reigns'. In lieu of specific gifts, stores urged customers to make presents of gift tokens, which could be exchanged once suitable gifts were back in the shops. Hubbards of Worthing, for example, said that its gift tokens could also be exchanged in no less than '65 associated businesses throughout the country, including London'. The government had its own twist on this and reminded people that opening savings accounts was the most patriotic expression of Christmas cheer. The *Sunday Post* ran an advertisement for the 'Scottish Savings Committee', which noted the difficulty of selecting presents for loved ones when things were still so scarce. But, said the advertisement, 'This need not raise serious difficulties – Gift Tokens is the answer, and it's the Gift that Grows … For man, woman or child they're equally welcome whatever their tastes, and will be appreciated by friends, or members of your staff … Gift Tokens are not only patriotic, they're practical.' Not only that, but they were easy to post and came with a free Christmas card in which the buyer could stick the National Savings Stamps.

As it had been before the war, a trip to meet Father Christmas in a local department store was an essential part of any lucky child's festivities. Just about every town and city in the nation had at least one incarnation of Santa in residence. In Stoke-on-Trent, he was hosted by Huntbach & Co, 'The House of Confidence', in Hanley, where he was joined by his 'charming little daughter' Chrissie Christmas. Open every day, except Thursdays, in the basement toy department, Father Christmas greeted youngsters whose parents could secure them a 'lucky parcel' for the sum of 1s (5p).

Sadly, it seemed, in wartime even Santa was tempted to occasionally break the law. Fulham resident Edward McMahon, dressed in full Father Christmas outfit, was arrested in Hyde Park for selling lighter wicks, contrary to regulations. McMahon, who had been carrying a banner reading, 'The age of folly', claimed, 'What I was offering was spiritual lighters.' He was discharged under the Probation of Offenders' Act.

For the law-abiding Santas, there were many trips to make to less fortunate children. For children with no parents to take them to department stores, Santa Claus came to them. The children of the Diocese Children's Home in Dundee were treated to a party, organised by the local Social Welfare Committee. Carol singing, games and even a cinema show were put on. Santa, played by Councillor Archibald Powrie, later Lord Provost of Dundee, gave each child a gift from under the 'gaily decorated' Christmas tree. Even those children who had fallen victim to an outbreak of measles and thus spent Yuletide being treated at King's Cross Hospital were guaranteed 'their gifts and dainties'.

In Burton upon Trent, some 2,273 children of servicemen and servicewomen, together with evacuees and orphans, were entertained over four days at the Town Hall, thanks to an appeal run by two local newspapers, the *Burton Daily Mail* and the *Burton Observer*. In the north-west of England, American soldiers hosted around a dozen parties, for 1,500 children from Cheshire and Lancashire, at the Air Services Command Base for that region. The GIs had spent months making presents, like model jeeps, racing cars, aeroplanes and trains, dolls and dolls' houses, Donald Ducks and prams, in their spare time and which they gave to evacuees and children of prisoners of war.

Combining a celebration of their stand down and Christmas, the Home Guard of C-Company, Eastbourne, held three functions. At one, held at the local Drill Hall, around 300 children were entertained with songs and games and given what the *Eastbourne Chronicle* called 'a splendid tea prepared for them by Baker Sons & Hyde with every conceivable delight in the way of cakes, rolls, sandwiches etc'. Entertainment came by way of local conjuror Albert Maas who 'baffled the children and mystified the grown-ups'. This was followed by games, competitions and 'a singsong which was heartily joined in by all the youngsters'.

In Hull, the Eastern Division of the Prisoner-of-War Relatives' Fellowship Committee held its own party at the works canteen of the Metal Box Company. Miss Alice Pickles and her pupils gave a concert and Father Christmas, played by chief warden R.G. Tarran, handed the children gifts made by the 'wardens and friends'. Each child also received an apple and a threepenny bit. Three-year-old Bruce Douglas, whose father had been a prisoner of war for three years, presented Mr Tarran with a bouquet of flowers for his wife, who was too busy making up care packages for prisoners of war to attend the celebration. ARP wardens in Belfast held their own children's party at which a film show, a variety performance and tea, including fruit and ice cream, were provided. On Christmas Day itself, local dignitaries, up and down the country, made visits to important institutions like the communities in Cardiff, Llanelly and Swansea where hospitals and residential homes received the attention of their local mayors.

With air raids largely at an end, blackout restrictions were eased, enabling carol singers to carry lanterns through the streets once more. With the prospect of invasion gone, churches were not only permitted to light up; for the first time in five years, they could also ring the bells.

On 2 December 1944, the *Daily Mirror*'s headline brought happy news: 'Home for Christmas: The First 2,000 Here.'

'Two thousand tough, sunburned veterans of the Mediterranean war' had been sent home to their families on 28 days' leave. The men had left a transit camp in 'a northern town' at 5am that morning and, as newspapers landed on doormats, were travelling by train to communities across the country. The leave had been arranged at short notice and, for their families, the first news of the joyful reunions would be an unexpected knock on the door from a son, a father, a husband or a brother.

Twenty-five-year-old Russell Ponting, a former counting house clerk from Swindon who was now serving as a sergeant in the RAMC, told reporters: 'We've lived Britain, dreamed Britain, spoke Britain and thought Britain all the time we've been away ... now we are here we do not know quite what to do, what to say. But we are home ... we will try to pick up the threads of our old life. Some of us will see our wives again, meet children we have known only by photographs. I'll try to get married ... No, I won't tell you her name. It might not come off. But whatever we do, we'll have the best Christmas in years.' Records indicate that Staff Sergeant Ponting, of 97 Curtis Street, Swindon, did indeed, marry his sweetheart, Kathleen Seager – listed in the 1939 register as a 'tobacco spikker' – in his hometown. A year later, he was awarded the British Empire Medal for his service in Italy.

A few days later, the *Essex Chronicle* reported on the Morley family of Great Baddow. The 'white-haired Mrs Morley' had no less than five sons serving their country. Two of them, Ted and Harry, who were both in the Essex Yeomanry, had now arrived home and their mother could not have been happier:

'I soon got the table laid … I heard myself murmuring "Thank the good Lord!" … I suppose there were a few tears as well, but they were tears of thankfulness … there was so much to say, in all the excitement we almost forgot about eating food!' Ted said that the beds, and their clean white sheets, were so comfortable that neither of the brothers could get much sleep. So, with their mother's help, the pair had remade their beds on the bedroom floor. 'And slept like tops.'

The *Sunday Post* told the story of Private John Devanney, who had been away from home for five years with the Chindits, the special operations units of the British and Indian armies, and had twice been posted as 'missing'. He surprised his parents by 'walking into the house' two weeks earlier than expected.

As well as thousands of returning servicemen, many evacuees, who had been sheltering away from the major towns and cities, were returned home to their families to celebrate Christmas. The *Kent and Sussex Courier* published a photograph of one batch of smiling youngsters arriving at Tunbridge Wells Central railway station from their temporary homes in the West Country.

With all these happy reunions, as Christmas approached, it now seemed that the British weather might disrupt the celebrations. A 90mph gale swept the south of Britain, sending 60ft (18.2m) waves crashing on to South Coast beaches. Then a horrible fog descended. The appalling weather cast doubt on many festivities, but, fortunately, at almost the last minute, it brightened up remarkably to provide 'sparkling sunshine' for many on 25 December.

All in all, as 1945 dawned, life seemed to be edging, albeit slowly, towards something resembling normality. On 27 December, the *Western Mail and South West News* declared it 'the best Christmas of the War'. As New Year revellers gathered, they could finally say with growing certainty that the war would be over by Christmas.

Chapter 14

King, Queen, Everyone Else … Are At One

*The children won't go without me. I won't leave the King. And the King will
never leave.*

Queen Elizabeth

Like all British women aged 16 or over, the king's eldest daughter
had registered for war service. In Princess Elizabeth's case, however,
it was initially deemed unlikely that she would fully participate. But
the princess had other ideas. Despite the reluctance of her father, in April
1945 she joined the Auxiliary Territorial Service (ATS), becoming No 230872
2nd Subaltern Elizabeth Windsor. Initially stationed at Aldershot, she was
later transferred to the Mechanical Transport Training Section at Camberley
and trained to drive heavy goods vehicles, and ambulances, as well as how
to maintain and repair them. Five months later, she was promoted to junior
commander, which was the equivalent of captain.

From the very beginning, the royals had aided the war effort. Engagements
by George VI, and by members of his family, had long proved important to the
nation's morale, particularly on the Home Front. Tours of munitions factories
or military units, and encouraging broadcasts to the Empire, had undoubtedly
lifted spirits. Cinema newsreels showing the king and queen at work did
much to cement in the public consciousness that, working class or aristocracy,
everyone was pulling together.

At least this was what the newsreels reminded everyone. Privately, of
course, some of those in the worst-hit towns and cities simply could not have
unqualified empathy with the monarch. Many of those in Hull, for example,
visited by the royal couple in August 1941, had lost everything in the Blitz. It
would be quite wrong to suggest that it went unnoticed that, even after royal
residences were bombed, unlike those of his subjects whose only home had
been destroyed, the king had several grand houses left undamaged. Even so,
the British people were in no doubt that their king and queen were doing their
best and were on their side. And none of them knew just how close the king
and queen had come to serious injury.

Buckingham Palace had first been attacked on 8 September 1940, the second
day of Germany's bombing campaign on Britain's southern towns and cities. A

50kg (110lb) delayed-action bomb fell on the Palace grounds. The following day, there was another. When that detonated, it destroyed much of the Palace's swimming pool and part of its north wing. On 13 September, there were three daytime raids on London. The second of these targeted Buckingham Palace. That night, American broadcaster Raymond Gram Swing told his listeners that 'the King and Queen were in the basement like the rest of London'. In fact, they were not. As the raid began, around 11am, the king and queen were drinking tea in their living quarters. In a letter to Queen Mary, the queen described what had happened:

'We heard the unmistakable whirr-whirr of a German plane. We said: "Ah, a German," and before anything else could be said, there was the noise of an aircraft diving at great speed, and then the scream of a bomb. It all happened so quickly, that we only had time to look foolishly at each other, when the scream hurtled past us, and exploded with a tremendous crash in the quadrangle. I saw a great column of smoke and earth thrown up into the air, and then we all ducked like lightning into the corridor. There was another tremendous explosion, and we and our two pages, who were outside the door, remained for a moment or two in the corridor, away from the staircase, in case of flying glass … then came a cry for "bandages" and the first-aid party rose magnificently to the occasion, and treated the three casualties calmly and correctly. How they survived I don't know.'

Outside, a court correspondent was leaving the Palace and witnessed the attack: '… a twin-engined plane was seen diving from the clouds … the pilot appeared to cut his engines and the machine lost speed. Then came the whistle of bombs, and explosions were heard in rapid succession …'

The attacker had dropped five high-explosive bombs on the Palace. Two of them struck the inner quadrangle, rupturing a water main and shattering hundreds of windows on the Palace's southern and western sides. One hit the Royal Chapel in the south wing, destroying it and injuring four workmen. One of them, Alfred Davies, was killed. The fourth bomb fell on to the Palace forecourt, and one in the road, in front of the Victoria Memorial, left a crater 30ft (9m) by 20ft (6m), some 10ft (3m) deep.

Details of just how close to harm the monarch and his wife had come was kept from the public. And, for a while, from Winston Churchill himself – the king had been certain that the prime minister would have insisted that they move out of London. Churchill later wrote, 'Had the windows been closed instead of open, the whole of the glass would have splintered into the faces of the King and Queen, causing terrible injuries. So little did they make of it that even I ... never realised until long afterwards ... what had actually happened.'

Regardless of their undoubted shock, after the all-clear sounded a couple of hours later, the king and queen visited East and West Ham where the situation was, of course, much worse. In her letter to her mother-in-law, the queen wrote that she felt as though she was 'walking in a dead city ... all the houses evacuated, and yet through the broken windows one saw all the poor little possessions, photographs, beds, just as they were left'.

Reports of the attack appeared in that evening's newspapers and, while they criticised its outrageous 'barbarous attack' on the monarch, the damage, and danger, was downplayed. The Ministry of Defence reported that only 'slight damage' had been suffered. Newspapers reported that, 'as they left the Palace, both the King and Queen appeared to be quite unshaken by their experience'.

Swing, the American broadcaster, noted that the bombing of Buckingham Palace was 'a great psychological blunder ... Tonight Britain is more unified than before that German bomber slid down over Buckingham Palace. Now they all have shared this ordeal, King, Queen and everyone else. They are one'.

In common with so many British families, the royal family had suffered personal loss during the war. In August 1942, the king's youngest-surviving brother, Prince George, the Duke of Kent, was killed in an air crash – the first English royal to die while on active service since Richard III fell in battle at Bosworth in 1485. After a career in the Royal Navy, and time spent as a civil servant, the duke had spent part of the war as rear admiral and then as an air commodore in the RAF. In the twelve months prior to his death, he had travelled some 40,000 miles (64,373km) visiting RAF stations in Britain, and a further 15,000 miles (24,000km) overseas. He had been on his way to inspect air bases in Iceland when the RAF Short Sunderland flying boat carrying the prince and fourteen others crashed into a hillside near Dunbeath, Caithness. All but one of the passengers died. The duke was thirty-nine years old, and left behind his widow, Marina, and three children, Edward – who inherited his title – Alexandra, and seven-week-old Michael.

His brother, Henry, the Duke of Gloucester, had been a career soldier, although he had retired from active service in 1937. Between 1939 and 1940, he had acted as Chief Liaison Officer to Lord Gort, Commander-in-Chief of the British Expeditionary Force. In 1940, he had come close to serious harm while driving through Tournai when he was caught up in heavy enemy bombing. He had escaped from his burning car but needed medical attention on a heavily-bleeding wound. After his brother's death, Henry was no longer risked in combat areas, and served as Chief Liaison Officer, GHQ Home Forces. In 1945, he was appointed Governor-General of Australia.

The King's nephew, George Lascelles – the son of the Princess Royal and the Earl of Harewood – had joined the Grenadier Guards in 1942, the regiment of which his cousin, Princess Elizabeth, was Colonel-in-Chief. He had served in North Africa and in Italy. Two days after the king's brief Normandy visit, Captain Lascelles was wounded and captured at Monte Corno and thereafter held as a prisoner at Oflag IV-C – Colditz. In March 1945, Hitler, no longer considering the VIP a useful bargaining chip, signed his death warrant. Fortunately for Lascelles, Gottlob Berger, the SS officer in charge of prison camps, realised that the war was all but over and refused to carry out the sentence. In May 1945, Lascelles was handed over to the Swiss.

The Duke of Windsor, meanwhile, had spent much of the war as Governor of the Bahamas, safely out of harm's reach, or anywhere his sympathies towards Germany might have any influence. In May 1945, he announced that he was resigning his post: 'Nearly five years in Nassau is the longest time I have spent in one place since my adolescence, and the longest I hope to spend in any place in the future. ... We have no immediate plan beyond going to New York and probably to my ranch in Canada.'

To those who wondered whether the duke's public service had ended, he said, 'My resignation does not mean a permanent severance from public life. After the war, men with experience will be badly needed, and I'll fit in anywhere that I can be helpful. ... I have interests in Canada, America and Europe. ... I shall go to England some day ...'

His duchess, Wallis, said: 'With the world as it is, one could not make a decision now. But we shall definitely visit France. Our possessions are scattered all over France. We must see what is left ...'

In late July 1944, the king made another of his visits to troops in Europe – this time to Italy, where he toured hundreds of miles of the front by road and air, reviewing thousands of British, Empire and Polish troops. He personally awarded a number of Victoria Crosses: to Lieutenant (Temporary Captain) Richard Wakeford of the Royal Hampshire Regiment; Fusilier Richard Arthur Jefferson of the Lancashire Fusiliers; and Sepoy Kamal Ram of the Gujars of Rajputana.

With the king abroad, Princess Elizabeth performed her first duties as a Counsellor of State, a position she had taken up the previous April, when she had turned eighteen. The Princess, together with the Queen, granted Royal Assents to acts passed through Parliament that included the Food and Drugs (Milk and Dairies) Act, and the Agricultural (Miscellaneous Provisions) Act. In October 1944, the king travelled once more to the Continent to visit Montgomery's headquarters in Eindhoven, where he knighted several senior officers – the first time a king had knighted soldiers on a battlefield since Henry V at Agincourt in 1415.

In February 1945, the king had yet another important investiture to perform. Harold Flintoff of Thunderhead Farm, Farndale in Yorkshire stood in front of the king at Buckingham Palace to receive his Edward Medal for stopping a runaway bull at the farm. He was just fourteen years old.

Chapter 15

Escape From Camp 198

Four German officers were seen late this afternoon at Kenfig Hill by Mr Richard Jones, a farmer. They were taking cover on the edge of a field. 'Come here!' Mr Jones shouted. They gave themselves up.

Daily Herald

Just before Christmas 1944, six escaped German prisoners of war were recaptured by two policemen and a Corporation bus driver outside the offices of the Derby Gas, Light and Coke Company in the home of the Rolls-Royce Merlin aero-engines that had powered the Spitfires and Hurricanes of the Battle of Britain and were now doing the same for the Avro Lancaster bombers pounding the Third Reich.

The Germans had escaped from a camp in Staffordshire, but their luck ran out when their stolen car broke down opposite Derby's main police station. After a short chase through the town centre, they were rounded up, the last one collared by a bus driver on his way to start the early shift.

Their fate was typical of the many German prisoners of war who attempted to escape from UK prison camps during the Second World War. They were usually ill-prepared for such a venture, and not one of them was ever at large for long before being rounded up, usually thoroughly miserable and glad to be back in what had become their home for the duration.

There was one escape attempt, however, that set in motion one of the biggest manhunts that the British mainland has ever seen, when seventy German prisoners of war escaped from their camp on the outskirts of Bridgend in Glamorgan.

Camp 198, known locally as Island Farm, had originally been built in 1938 to house female munitions workers at the nearby Waterton Royal Ordnance factory, but conditions there were so basic that the hostel was soon lying empty, the women preferring to travel daily from their own homes, even though that often involved an hour-long journey to work. From 1943, American soldiers of the 10th Infantry Regiment were housed at Island Farm to await the Allied invasion of France. After D-Day, camps were needed to house the thousands of German, Italian and Ukrainian prisoners of war captured as the Axis crumbled. Island Farm became one of them, its prefabricated concrete huts now converted and surrounded by barbed wire fences rather than open fields. It housed 1,600 German officers, and some of them soon turned their attention to escaping.

In January 1945, camp guards discovered a tunnel. It was one of two started by the prisoners but their guards either did not look for another, or, if they did, could not find one. Thus, work on the second tunnel, started in Hut 9, continued until, at 30ft (9.1m), it drove under a perimeter fence. The tunnel was about 3ft wide, and some 4–5ft (about 1.5m) below ground, much of it going under a concrete path. Ordinarily, soil might have been disposed of by being dumped in vegetable plots – but it was still winter and so the heavy clay, orange in colour, was shaped into balls and hidden behind a false wall constructed in Hut 9. The tunnel was supported by wood that the prisoners had managed to salvage. When supplies ran out, they cut down their bed legs. And used bed boards to help shore up the tunnel. A ventilation pipe was made from condensed milk tins and manually operated by a makeshift bellows. Lighting was tapped off the main electricity supply.

At around 10pm on Saturday, 10 March 1945, everything was ready. The escapees divided themselves into small groups, each with a rough map, a home-made compass and whatever food they had managed to store ready for their bid for freedom. Fake identity papers purported to show that the men were Norwegian engineers.

In some ways, Camp 198 was still only a work in progress. There were no sentry towers and there was no effective perimeter lighting. Aided by all that, and the noise coming from a camp concert, seventy men were able to make their escape before the alarm was raised at around 4am on the Sunday morning. Fourteen others were soon recaptured, but now there was a countrywide manhunt for the rest.

Newspapers kept the British public up-to-date with progress made in recapturing the prisoners from Camp 198. There were some colourful accounts. One said that a group stole a car belonging to a local doctor and, when it would not start, they enlisted the help of three British soldiers who were passing by.

The *Western Mail* reported,

'A woman's wit beat three of the escaped Nazis on Wednesday evening and resulted in their capture while having a cup of tea … The suspicions of a farmer's wife, Mrs Elizabeth Davies, were aroused when a man in dark clothing called at her farm and inquired the way to Swansea. She at once invited the man in to have a cup of tea, but he demurred, saying he had two friends outside. Mrs Davies then invited him to bring the others along too. The invitation was accepted, and the three men went into the farmhouse. The farmer's wife busied herself preparing tea, walking in and out of the room to prepare the meal. While she was doing this, however, she was getting into touch with other people to fetch the police. While help was arriving, she kept the Nazis entertained and in a very few minutes, instead of being on their way to Swansea, they were making the journey back to Bridgend. The men must have been lurking in the dense woods which surround Margam Castle, or upon Margam mountain, while continuous searches went on for them on previous days. Six men were recaptured during Tuesday night, two being caught at Chepstow, three at Glynneath, and one at Neath.'

A workers' bus from Melincourt was coming from Cwmgwrach when the driver, Gwyn Lewis, a member of the Glamorgan Special Constabulary, saw four men creeping along the hedgerows. He told his three passengers and they alighted from the bus and captured one man apiece. The prisoners were taken to Glynneath police station in the bus. 'They were docile in their attitude and hungry and unkempt, and seemed glad that their period of freedom had ended.' The fourth man escaped and boarded a mineral train going in the direction of Neath. Messages were sent through to the area, and PC Butler, on duty at Aberdulais railway station, flashed his light on the passing train and saw a man riding between two wagons. He shouted to the guard and then telephoned Neath. The military and the police were awaiting the man's arrival at Neath Riverside station. A shunter on the Great Western Railway who witnessed his arrest told reporters that, when the man got out, he said, 'German prisoner. Is this Cardiff?'

Many resources were used to recapture the prisoners. Low-flying aircraft maintained observation on woods and less frequented country roads, and pilots were kept in touch by wireless with the RAF and police road controls. The airmen had been instrumental in the recapture of several of the Germans. Specially trained Alsatians had been used by the military in keeping up the search after nightfall, and the Metropolitan Police helped railway police by scrutinising passengers arriving in London from South Wales, while a close watch was kept at all Welsh railway stations and ports.

The *Western Mail* also reported, 'Three prisoners recaptured in the Aberdare Valley about 2am Thursday morning were taken by War Department constable William Edward Williams ... He was on duty outside the gates of a factory when he saw the shadowy outlines of three men approaching. He called to them to stop but they did not do so. But, challenged again, they halted. He discovered by the light of his torch that they were Germans, only one of whom could speak halting English. They had travelled over the Rhondda mountains from Bridgend along the Treherbert road. One of them had been decorated with the Iron Cross first-class, and a second man with the Iron Cross second-class. They were docile, and had in their possession a quantity of currents, raisins, margarine, and also rough maps of the district sketched on their pocket handkerchiefs.'

The *Daily Herald*: 'Forty-three of the seventy Germans who escaped from a prison camp yesterday have been recaptured. There were two picked up tonight by special constables within 200yd of Kenfig Hill police station, about 7 miles [11.2km] from the camp. Three more were found by war reserve police near a factory at Pencoed, 3.5 miles [5.6km] east of Bridgend.

'The vast game of hide and seek, led by thousands of armed troops, goes on. Efforts to get away from South Wales by sea have been anticipated by a close watch at every port. The need for this was proved today. Two men were recaptured by a mobile policeman at Culverhouse Cross on the outskirts of Cardiff, after a 15-mile [24km] cross country trek ...

'Throughout the day, farm labourers and land girls, wielding pitchforks, probed the quiet lanes and hedgerows of the Valley of Glamorgan, while low-flying spotter planes zoomed and dipped above them ... A check by the military authorities in the area has established that no arms are missing from the camp.'

The *West Sussex Gazette* reported that two of the German prisoners had been recaptured at Eastleigh four days later. A railway shunter saw a man leave a railway wagon in the goods yard about 6am. Later, some kit bearing the name and number of a German officer prisoner was found on a train arriving from South Wales. The wagon revealed signs that someone, probably two men, had lived in it for several days. A cordon was thrown around the goods yard and the police were helped by railway employees in a widespread search. During the morning a German lieutenant and a sergeant were found hiding in a cement truck. They offered no resistance and were taken to the police station until they were sent back to Bridgend.

The *Leicester Evening Mail* told of a local hero: 'Former Leicestershire police constable John Hopkins, who had played rugby for Leicester Tigers in the 1935–36 season when he was stationed at Coalville, showed his old burst of speed in a 100-yard sprint which ended in his capturing the last three of the seventy German prisoners who escaped from Bridgend camp. Hopkins, now farming at Cwmcyrnach Farm, some 30 miles [48km] from Bridgend, made his captures at Glais, near Swansea, after a search for men who accosted his wife and mother on a mountain path on Saturday night.

'Hopkins found the three men and asked to see their passes. They immediately made off, but he chased and caught them. When he caught up with them at the end of the short sprint, they told him it was "good sport". Hopkins took his prisoners to the police station but, finding no-one there, then took them to the local post office. They were later taken back to their camp. The men, who had a few squares of toast and some sweets in their possession, told Hopkins they had been roaming the mountains.'

The *Hartlepool Northern Daily Mail*: 'Only three German prisoners of war out of the original seventy who escaped from camp at Bridgend on Sunday are now at liberty. Early this morning, four were spotted by police on the road at Cymmer, Port Talbot, and invited to come along to the station – a request they were only too glad to obey. The four prisoners recaptured early today had a narrow escape from death. They had left the mountain track in the dark and were only a few yards from one of the most treacherous bogs in South Wales. Inspector E.J. Hunter, leading the police in the search, picked the men out with his electric torch and warned them of their danger. They made quiet surrender.'

The *Dundee Courier*:

'Out of the seventy prisoners who escaped from the Bridgend, Glamorgan, camp, all but seven have been recaptured. Two were found at Eastleigh, Hants, goods yard in a cement wagon from South Wales. Three gave themselves up to a police patrol near Aberdare. Four were caught at Castle Bromwich, Warwickshire. A man – Section Leader Tomlinson – out with his gun in some woods, found them asleep. Three spoke English. They said that on the day of the breakout they took a car and got into Gloucestershire, where they abandoned it. They made their way to Castle Bromwich by goods trains.'

A Glamorgan police official said they had received reports from farmers around Bridgend of cows which had no milk to give at milking time. It was fairly obvious, he said, that escaped prisoners of war were milking cows to satisfy their thirst.

In March 1945 alone, there were reports of other escape attempts. Herbert Lizzars, a 21-year-old German prisoner of war, was spotted breaking out of a camp in County Tyrone at 10.30pm on 19 March. Refusing to halt, Lizzars was fired upon by a sentry, receiving four bullet wounds in the right arm, which was shattered, and a fifth wound to the chest. Two German military doctors attached to the camp took him by lorry to Dungannon hospital, where he was given blood transfusions and later transferred to Belfast.

Two German paratroopers who escaped from a working party in Hertfordshire were caught hiding in a spinney not far from where they escaped and, in Lanarkshire, three German prisoners of war were recaptured in a field about 20 miles [32km] from their camp. According to reports, 'they were exhausted'.

Occasionally, some were killed while making their break for freedom. Two German prisoners of war were shot dead when trying to escape from an American camp at Sudbury, between Burton upon Trent and Uttoxeter. Ten men were involved in the escape and, in addition to those who were shot, all the others were recaptured soon afterwards.

A Luftwaffe prisoner of war who was shot while attempting to escape from Lodge Moor camp near Sheffield died in the local Wharncliffe Hospital. Seen in the early morning at the wire surrounding the camp, when he did not obey an order to stop, a guard opened fire.

The *Yorkshire Post* reported, 'Two escaped German prisoners of war were recaptured yesterday from a wagon in the LMS goods yard, Bridge Street, Bradford, by railway employees. The chief foreman, Mr A.M. Payne, said that, when he arrived at the yard, a wrestling match was in progress between two members of his staff and the two Germans. One of them was inclined to be truculent, but Mr Payne overcame him and sent for the police. Confirming the recapture, Chief Inspector Rushworth of the Bradford City police, said the two men did not belong to the seventy who escaped from Wales.'

That month, ninety-four Italian prisoners of war on land drainage work in North Wales went on strike in support of a demand for a reduction in working time from fifty-two to forty-eight hours a week. The men barricaded themselves in a hut in their camp and did not give in until a detachment of soldiers was called in seven days later. On 21 March 1945, Sir James Grigg, the War Minister, told the House of Commons that over 97 per cent of the Italian prisoners of war in Britain and 25 per cent of the Germans were usefully employed. Asked if it was not possible, in view of the shortage of manpower, to employ more of the Germans, Sir James replied, 'One of the reasons why there are a number of escapes is that we attempt to use them on useful work where they cannot be guarded 100 per cent. Remember what is the relative value of the work performed by the Germans on the one hand and the Italians on the other? I have the information, but wild horses would not drag it out of me.' The minister added that 420 German prisoners of war had escaped from the camps in Britain so far, and four were still at large.

After the March 1945 escape, Camp 198 was closed and its inmates transferred to Camp 181 in Worksop, Nottinghamshire. It was then redesignated as Special Camp XI and used to house high-ranking German officers, some of them destined to face war crimes trials, before being closed altogether in May 1948.

Chapter 16

Flying Over a Sheet of Fire

We did not recognise our street anymore. Fire, only fire wherever we looked ...
there were burning vehicles and carts with refugees, people, horses, all of them
screaming and shouting in fear of death ...

Lothar Metzger, Dresden resident

Even in war, if at all possible, some kind of 'normality' has to be preserved. Thus, on 18 June 1944, less than two weeks after the Normandy landings, the Deutscher Fussball-Bund – the German Football Association – pressed on with its national play-off final in Berlin. The 70,000 spectators who saw Dresdner SC beat the Luftwaffe club, LSV Hamburg, might have been told that, a few days earlier, the first V-1 rocket had landed in Britain. They would have been unaware, however, that, at the very moment they were filing into the Olympic Stadium, at Cherbourg the German garrison had been encircled by American forces. Dresdner SC won easily, 4–0, their last goal scored by 28-year-old Dresden-born Helmut Schön, who, as a schoolboy, had taken up the game in the streets of his home city, despite the objections of his art dealer father who regarded the game as too 'working class'.

In February 1945, Schön had much more on his mind than the result of a football match. He was on duty as a factory air-raid warden in Dresden when the Allies firebombed the city known as 'the Florence of the Elbe'. It was an event that many would later say amounted to nothing less than a war crime. In four separate raids by more than 1,200 British and American bombers, some eight square miles of this most beautiful Saxon city were left in ruins, 75,000 homes were destroyed and, according to a report by the Historical Commission on the Aerial Bombing of Dresden, published on behalf of the city in 2010, up to 25,000 people were killed. That figure has often been claimed to be much larger, sometimes running into six figures, not least because no-one knows how many refugees had fled to Dresden from the Soviet advance into Silesia. However, the commission's exhaustive research found no 'sustainable arguments which placed the result in doubt'. Whatever the final total of deaths, the terrifying destruction of Dresden was one of the most controversial Allied actions of the war, and the culmination of a campaign that has been viewed in many quarters as morally indefensible, and not just with the benefit of hindsight.

The indiscriminate bombing of German cities had been going on since February 1942. Hitherto, raids had concentrated on bridges, railway marshalling yards and other key infrastructure, but they had proved largely ineffective in stalling the Nazi war machine. Now the RAF switched to 'area bombing', night-time blanket attacks on cities and other urban areas. It was designed to both degrade German industry and to break civilian morale. The British Cabinet was persuaded that area bombing could shorten the war, and perhaps even render an invasion of Europe unnecessary, thus preventing a possible repeat of the brutal and costly trench warfare of the First World War.

The new head of Bomber Command, Air Marshall Arthur Harris, would soon earn his nickname of 'Bomber'. Harris was a keen advocate of the 'dehousing of the German workforce' by sending 1,000 bombers nightly to destroy great industrial cities in a matter of hours. On the night of 30–31 May 1942, the RAF launched the first 1,000-bomber raid of Operation Millennium when 1,047 aircraft dropped more than 2,000 tons (1814.3 tonnes) of bombs on Cologne, Germany's third-largest city, destroying 13,000 buildings, including more than 2,500 industrial sites. The fire brigade reported 2,500 separate fires, 1,700 of them classed as 'large'. Remarkably, only 500 people were killed, but a further 5,000 were injured and more than 45,000 were 'dehoused' – bombed out of their homes.

The force was two and half times larger than any previous single air raid by the RAF. Forty-one aircraft were lost, the highest number for a single night since thirty-seven failed to return home in November 1941 after raids on Berlin, Cologne and Mannheim. Putting together such a force had been no easy task, but it was eventually achieved by using every spare aircraft capable of taking part in such an operation, and every available aircrew. And that was how Operation Millennium continued. Initially, the workhorse of the operation was the pre-war Vickers Wellington bomber, but, in the second half of 1942, the Avro Lancaster became widely available and was soon on its way to becoming the most famous and successful British heavy bomber of the war, In August 1942, the Americans introduced their B-17 'Flying Fortress' bombers.

Soon the raids were around the clock, the RAF attacking by night and the US Army Air Force, flying from British bases, in daylight, although after sixty B-17s were lost (another seventeen were so badly damaged that they had to be scrapped) on a raid on ball-bearing factories at Schweinfurt in October 1943, daylight raids were put on hold until 1944, when long-distance fighter escorts became available.

The figure of '1,000 bombers' was newsworthy, the stuff of morale-boosting headlines for the British Press. After the Cologne raid of May 1942, 'One Bomber Every Six Seconds' screamed the *Daily Express*. It was big news across the Atlantic, too: '1,000 British Bombers Set Cologne On Fire' was the front-page headline on the *New York Times*.

Night raids continued unabated. In late July into August 1943, in Operation Gomorrah, a joint raid by British and American bombers, Hamburg, Germany's second-largest city, was attacked relentlessly for a whole week. More than 60 per cent of the city's housing was destroyed, and an estimated 40,000 of its citizens were killed. Berlin, Hamburg, Frankfurt, Munich, Stuttgart – the list went on as the final three months of 1944 saw the Allies enjoy complete air supremacy in North-West Europe. No important German city or town escaped. Then the focus moved to the east. In order to halt German troop movements and to aid its advance on the German capital, the Soviet Union requested raids on targets that included Berlin, Leipzig, Chemnitz – and Dresden. On 3 February, an estimated 25,000 Berliners were killed during a raid by 1,000 American bombers. Ten days later, it was Dresden's turn again. The city had been bombed twice before, in October 1944 when the US Army Air Force had attacked marshalling yards, killing scores of workers but leaving the city itself relatively unscathed.

To many, Dresden was no more than a cultural city with its Semper Gallery containing works by Rembrandt, Raphael, Titian and Van Dyck; the Zwinger palatial complex, which was one of the most important Baroque buildings in Germany; the eighteenth-century Lutheran Frauenkirche (Church of Our Lady); and its connections with Romantic composers Richard Wagner and Carl Maria von Weber.

When reports of the third raid on Dresden began to appear in British newspapers, the *Nottingham Evening Post*'s 'Echoes from Town' London correspondent wrote,

'It is difficult not to associate Dresden, now being bombed, with exquisite china rather than with war production. Shortly before the war broke out, a friend invited by the German government to tour the country with the party, visited Dresden and there picked up the most delightful little Dresden figure I have seen. The tiny Dresden lady, all frilly petticoats which looked like the finest handmade lace, was presented to me and lived with other treasures on a special shelf. Came the Blitz of 1940 and the ruin of my home, especially the room where the treasures were kept. No glass, no china was left, save the Dresden lady who continued to sit, undamaged and unperturbed, amidst the debris left by her countrymen.'

The *Daily Dispatch* reported,

'The Opera House where most of Richard Strauss's operas had their first night was totally destroyed. Irreplaceable art treasures have been transformed into smoking, pulverised rubble. The town – with the most beautiful buildings of the Baroque period, the most famous European collections of chinaware, and museums containing world famous art treasures – has gone for ever.'

The Allies, meanwhile, pointed out the presence of the Zeiss-Ikon optical factory and Siemans glass factory that manufactured gun sights, as well as factories producing radar, anti-aircraft shell fuses, gas masks and even engines for fighter aircraft. Another argument was that Dresden was a major communications centre and transportation hub for sending troops by rail and by road to face the Soviet advance.

The *Liverpool Daily Post's* 'London Letter' columnist agreed: 'Warlike Germany made a vital military centre of Dresden, now experiencing the double fury of Allied bombing and Russian guns.'

The *Daily Herald* said,

'The day and night raids on Dresden have done more than anything else to breakdown German administration, for it was to Dresden that the Nazis had shifted most of their vital files and documents. Now Dresden, a battered city, without telephone, telegraph or rail communications, is completely isolated from the rest of Germany, particularly from the Nazis' nerves centre, Berlin.'

Daily Record reporter Cyril Marshall wrote from Stockholm, 'Consternation has been caused among the Nazi leaders by the air destruction of Dresden. The Nazis had made all preparations to transfer the seat of government there when Berlin became untenable.'

By now, Dresden had been turned into a dystopian necropolis of charred and suffocated bodies. Dresden is 'one great field of ruins' said the German-controlled Scandinavian Telegram Bureau. The Swedish newspaper *Dagens Nyheter* reported, 'Dresden was turned into one huge inferno when tens of thousands of refugees from Eastern Germany were killed.'

Previous raids bore no comparison to what unfolded on the night of 13 February 1945. The first aircraft to appear over Dresden late that evening were RAF Lancasters – a planned daylight raid by the Americans had been called off due to unsuitable weather conditions – and, meeting little opposition, they dropped their high-explosive bombs and incendiaries on a city centre comprised mostly of brick, sandstone and wood. The incendiaries started hundreds of small fires while the high-explosives flattened buildings and cratered streets, forcing firefighters to take cover and leave the fires to grow. It took this first wave of Lancasters only about fifteen minutes to unload their deadly cargo. Two and a half hours later, a second force of Lancasters arrived over Dresden, in number some 550 aircraft, twice the size of the first wave. The city was already in the grip of a firestorm with a ferocious wind – 'a hurricane' according to some survivors – tearing through the streets. The Lancasters dropped more bombs, more incendiaries. Some people were simply obliterated, reduced to atoms. Many more, probably the majority, suffocated in the carbon monoxide as the fires sucked oxygen from the air.

At noon the following day, more than 300 B-17s continued the bombing of Dresden. Through columns of smoke, still rising 15,000ft into the sky, they found it difficult to locate their targets. They managed to bomb some marshalling yards, while yet more residential areas were hit. And still Dresden's torment was not over. The next day, 15 February, more than 200 B-17s unloaded bombs meant for an oil plant near Leipzig when bad weather over their original target saw them switch to Dresden.

The city was still burning when the B-17s returned on 2 March, looking to bomb more marshalling yards and other industrial targets. On 7 April, they came back yet again, hitting similar targets.

For several months after the February raids, Dresden was a 'city of the dead'. Fear of disease saw thousands of corpses cremated on makeshift funeral pyres. Others were buried in mass graves. Allied prisoners were forced to extract bodies from huge piles of rubble. In 2020, Victor Gregg, a British paratrooper who had been captured at Arnhem and who was forced to work in a labour camp near Dresden, told *inews.co.uk*, 'It's the nature of the way people died. Boiled to death in water that they climbed in, roasted to death alive. They were burning alive in the streets, which to me nobody can offer an excuse.'

He was not the only one to wonder how on earth such a thing could have been allowed to happen. Roy Akehurst, an RAF wireless operator who had been involved in the attack, said later, 'It struck me at the time, the thought of the women and children down there. We seemed to fly for hours over a sheet of fire – a terrific red glow with thin haze over it. I found myself making comments to the crew: "Oh God, those poor people." It was completely uncalled for. You can't justify it.'

Survivor Margaret Freyer wrote in *The Bombing of Dresden*, 'What I saw is so horrific … Dead, dead, dead everywhere. Some completely black, like charcoal. Others completely untouched, lying as if they were asleep. Women in aprons, women with children sitting in the trams as if they had just nodded off … almost all of them naked. Some clinging to each other in groups as if they were clawing at each other …'

It is difficult to qualify what contribution the Allied area bombing campaign made to winning the war, especially its effectiveness on civilian morale. Despite the fact that some 400,000 civilians were killed by Allied bombing, it is argued that public support for the Nazi regime did not significantly alter. RAF Bomber Command – which dropped almost one million tonnes of explosives during 390,000 operations – and the US Eighth Air Force certainly paid a very high price. Sixty per cent of British bomber aircrews lost their lives, the highest casualty rate of any service during the Second World War.

In 1966, twenty-one years after he had witnessed such unimaginable horrors, football manager Helmut Schön's West German team lost to England in the World Cup Final. In 1974, his team won the trophy against Holland. Schön was very much a post-war European. He never blamed the Allies for the destruction of the city of his birth, preferring instead to direct his anger at the futility of war in general.

Chapter 17

Yalta – Unfinished Business?

A new generation will come which did not experience the horrors of war …
We have now to build up such a status, such a plan, that we can put as many
obstacles as possible to the coming generation quarrelling among themselves.
Winston Churchill

On Tuesday, 13 February 1945, the German News Agency raged: 'The destructive madness of Germany's enemies has now taken on final shape.' It was not referring to that day's firebombing of Dresden, however. Under the headlines 'Germany to be destroyed by the hateful plan of Yalta' and 'Chief war criminals, Churchill, Roosevelt and Stalin, agree on new crime to humanity', the agency wired the following:

'The Yalta plan is the biggest political murder attempt of all time. It aims straight at the German people, and, by its fiendish intention to exterminate the centre of Europe, hits the whole continent. Every line breezed the spirit of Morgenthau [Hans Morgenthau, the German-born American political scientist whose plan was to destroy post-war German industries that were key to military strength] and the notorious German hater Vansittart [Robert Vansittart, first secretary to the British delegation at the Versailles Peace Conference, and a staunch opponent of appeasement].'

The first German radio comment came later that day, from Zeesen, a small village a few kilometres from Berlin that was home to a facility for longwave broadcasting. In English it said, 'The communique reveals first of all that the Allies are in complete agreement concerning their plans of hate and destruction towards Germany. However, all the problems were left more or less pending so that the three powers can continue to present an artificially united front. Moscow, London and Washington reserve the right for themselves of forcing a government of which they approve on any and every country.

'The language used in reference to Germany appears in terminology that applied to uncivilised tribes … Germany is to be beaten by brute force, then it will be cut into pieces. All German industry will be carried off, and courts will be set to organise the mass murder of German men, women and children. Those Germans who survive will be pressed into slave gangs for the alien tyrants. This, in short, is the contents of the hate plan which is headed by the slogan "Unconditional surrender". Our forecast that our enemies are aiming at a super-Versailles is now definitely confirmed. The news of the Yalta plan is passing through Germany like a cry of alarm. Never shall this murder plan become reality. Our wrath shall rise to a national frenzy. Ninety million Germans will cling to the soil of their Fatherland and smash the most fiendish plan of all times by force of arms.'

Thus was the Nazi reaction to news coming from the meeting between the British prime minister, Winston Churchill, the US president, Franklin D. Roosevelt, and the Soviet premier, Joseph Stalin, that had just ended in the Russian resort town in the Crimea.

As a means of establishing a combined overall strategy for Europe once the war was won, the first conference between the leaders of the three Allied powers had been held in November 1943, when Churchill, Roosevelt and Stalin met in the Iranian capital, Tehran (Churchill had met with them separately, but this was the first time that Roosevelt and Stalin had been face to face). Meetings between Churchill and Roosevelt had been held as early as May 1940. Stalin had been invited to meet with them in Casablanca in January 1943, but refused, saying that he was busy with operations around Stalingrad. There, the British and American leaders had discussed the opening of a second front in Europe, the British looking at the southern part of the continent, the Americans favouring a cross-Channel invasion that Churchill regarded as premature. In Tehran, the opening of the hotly-debated European second front, and the timing of Soviet entry into the war in the Far East, were discussed, together with the design for a new organisation to replace the League of Nations and deliver and maintain international peace in a post-war world.

By the time the three world leaders met for a second time, in Yalta, the Americans and British were closing in on the Rhine, the Soviets were making progress in the east and victory in Europe was in sight. It was time to focus on the reorganisation of the continent once Germany was defeated. The Allies reiterated their plan: Germany would be forced into unconditional surrender and would then be divided into zones of occupation (including one administered by France, which was not represented at these meetings), after which there would be total de-Nazification, and the bringing to trial of those responsible for war crimes, for which there was growing and overwhelming evidence as the Allies advanced further.

The Americans and British agreed that future governments of nations bordering the Soviet Union should be 'friendly' towards it, while the Soviets agreed to allow free elections in all territories liberated from Nazi Germany. The reality was that, given the Soviet military domination of Eastern Europe, there was little that the Western Allies could do to prevent what would amount to a Soviet-sponsored government of Poland.

But, if the war in Europe was nearing its end, the Allies were much less certain of the war in the Pacific where the United States in particular were suffering heavy losses. It was agreed that, in return for its joining in the war against Japan within three months of Germany's defeat, the Soviet Union would be granted territorial concessions in the Far East. Roosevelt did not live to see the outcome. He died on 12 April 1945, his final legacy, according to his strongest critics, that he had handed to the Soviet Union Eastern Europe and North-East Asia 'on a plate'.

World reaction to the Yalta conference was inevitably varied. In Moscow, *Pravda* said, 'The freedom loving peoples of the world are vitally interested in seeing the great alliance of democratic powers which saved humanity from the German Fascist fiends, now finish off Hitlerite Germany rapidly and decisively and establish a strong edifice of peace and post-war security. The Allied armies, navies and air forces will strike new and more powerful blows at the heart of Germany, at times agreed upon by perfect understanding. This will shorten the length of the war. Nazi Germany is doomed. Her resistance is hopeless …'

The *New York Times*, reporting on the mood in Washington, said, 'What really interests the capital are the things which the Big Three statement did not even mention, and the first of these is Japan. There is some reticence here about hasty conclusions, but there has been growing confidence that Russia will participate in the war against Japan, and the selection of this particular date is described here as a remarkable coincidence, an intriguing bit of political warfare or an indication of great events to come.'

The 'Big Three announcement' was roundly denounced at a dinner of the co-ordinating committee of American Polish Associations in Washington. A statement issued on behalf of the association directors said that it constituted 'a fifth partition of the country' and the adjustments to the Curzon Line [the border between Soviet Russia and Poland established by the Paris Peace Conference on 8 December 1919, and later named after the British Foreign Secretary, George Nathaniel Curzon] were 'insulting concessions'. The *New York Times* felt that 'the Polish decision is a compromise which will have to be accepted on all sides as the best that can be obtained in the present troubled world'.

In London, members of the Polish government-in-exile met to decide whether they would co-operate with the Polish provisional government in occupied Warsaw, and with other Poles inside and outside Poland, in the new Polish Provisional Government of Unity. 'Should they refuse,' wrote the Press Association's diplomatic correspondent, Frank A. King, 'it seems possible that both Britain and America would withdraw recognition from the Polish London Government.' King's words were prescient: Britain and the United States would do so in July 1945.

Right from the Nazi invasion of Poland in September 1939, the catalyst for the Second World War, the country's story had been a tragic one. By the end of 1940, the Nazis had forcibly removed 80,000 Gentile Poles from the Jewish quarter of Warsaw and replaced them with 150,000 Jews who had been living elsewhere in the city. During the next two years, 100,000 of Warsaw's Jews had died, either from disease, starvation or execution, while a further 300,000 were transported to concentration camps to be exterminated. Himmler's plan was to make Warsaw 'Jew-free' by 20 April 1943, Hitler's fifty-fourth birthday. The Jews resisted and the Germans, sustaining substantial casualties, were forced to retreat, leaving behind their weapons and their dead. But some 60,000 Jews had also perished, leaving, it is believed, only 100 survivors of the first 'Warsaw Uprising'.

On 1 August 1944, the Armia Krajowa (the Polish Home Army, the largest underground resistance force in Occupied Europe), encouraged by the fact that the Red Army had reached the River Vistula, attacked German forces in Warsaw. The AK, as it was known, supported the Polish government-in-exile in London, and in this second uprising it enjoyed initial success. But the anticipated support from the Soviets did not materialise.

On 18 August, the Jewish Bund (a secular Jewish socialist movement) in Warsaw had pleaded with the Allies: 'For 18 days the population of Warsaw has carried on an unequal struggle against the barbarian aggressor, and with all Warsaw the remnants of Jewish youth are fighting. We are battling for our own common Polish cause against the enemy. Do all in your power to get help sent as soon as possible.'

Help was not forthcoming. The Soviets prevented the Western Allies from supplying the Poles from air bases in Soviet-controlled territory, and they disarmed AK fighters en route to Warsaw to join the struggle. Against a better armed and better supplied German force, Polish resistance and civilians alike were slaughtered in brutal fighting that saw dreadful atrocities committed by the SS. By the end of September 1944, now with no arms, food or water, the Poles were forced to give up the fight and, when, in January 1945, the Red Army entered Warsaw they found much of the city razed to the ground and learned that more than one million of its pre-war population had died at the hands of the Nazis. The hope that the AK could have gained control of Warsaw before the Soviet-backed Polish Committee of National Liberation, more commonly known as the Lublin Committee (it was proclaimed in Lublin, the largest Polish city east of the Vistula, on 22 July 1944), which functioned in direct opposition to the London-based government-in-exile, was a hopeless one. Stalin had encouraged the uprising and then watched on while the only properly organised Polish force that might have opposed Soviet occupation was destroyed.

In a letter to the *Western Morning News* on 27 February 1945, Sir Thomas Carew, whose ancestors had supported the Royalists during the English Civil War, said,

'If the proposed vote of confidence in the House of Commons takes the form of approving of the complete surrender to militant Bolshevism … it is to be hoped that a sufficient number of Members will have the courage to vote against it to defeat it. Whatever the consequences, they cannot be worse than announcing to the world that the British House of Commons associates itself with what is going on in Eastern Europe.'

That same day, Winston Churchill addressed the Commons at the beginning of a three-day debate. During a 110-minute speech, he updated MPs on various matters including the future of Poland, telling the House that his impression was 'that Marshal Stalin and the Soviet leaders wish to live in honourable friendship and equality with the Western democracies. I feel also that their word is their bond'.

He concluded by speaking about the plans for a new international organisation to maintain peace and security after the war's end:

'I suppose that during these last three winter months the human race all the world over have undergone more physical agony and misery than at any other period through which this planet has passed. In the Stone Age the numbers were fewer and the primitive creatures, little removed from their animal origin, knew no better. We suffer more. We feel more, I must admit in this war I never felt so grave a sense of responsibility as I did at Yalta. In 1940 and 1941, when we in this island were all alone and invasion was so near, the actual steps we ought to take and our attitude towards them seemed plain and simple. If a man is coming across the sea to kill you, you do everything in your power to make sure he dies before he finishes his journey. That may be difficult, and it may be painful, but at least it is simple. Now we enter into a world of imponderables and every stage self-questioning arises. It is a mistake to look too far ahead. Only one link in the chain of destiny can be handled at a time.

'I trust the House will feel that hope has been powerfully strengthened by our meeting in the Crimea. The ties that bind the three great powers together, and their mutual comprehension of each other, have grown. The United States has entered deeply and constructively into the life and salvation of Europe. We have all three set our hands to far-reaching engagements at once practical and solemn. United we have the unchallengeable power to lead the world to prosperity, freedom and happiness. The great powers must seek to serve and not to rule. Joined with other states, both large and small, we may found a world organisation which, armed with ample power, will guard the rights of all states, great or small, from aggression, or from the gathering of the means of aggression. I am sure that a fairer choice is open to mankind than they have known in recorded ages. The lights burn brighter and shine more broadly than before. Let us walk forward together.'

In 1985, President Ronald Reagan said, 'Why is Yalta important today? Not because we in the West want to reopen old disputes over boundaries; far from it. The reason Yalta remains important is that the freedom of Europe is unfinished business …'

It has been argued that conceding Eastern Europe to Stalin had effectively been settled at the Tehran conference, and that Yalta had merely seen a failed attempt by the Western Allies to rein back some kind of freedom for lands that would now be under Soviet control.

Whatever, the last of the three major conferences of the war would take place at Potsdam, 22 miles (35km) south-west of Berlin between 17 July and 2 August 1945. President Harry Truman would now represent the United States, while Britain would field two prime ministers, Clement Attlee succeeding Winston Churchill halfway through the conference. The redrawing of some European borders would be finally agreed, and Japan's unconditional surrender would be demanded, otherwise the country would meet its 'prompt and utter destruction'.

Chapter 18

Nothing That Dante Could Conceive ...

Arrogant German SS guards, who are being disarmed by British soldiers, claim that they had not the fuel to burn the bodies, nor time to bury them.

Colin Willis

In April 1945, Royal Army Medical Corps nursing orderly Tim Ward was given a week's leave from his unit, the 153rd Field Ambulance, which was attached to the 15th (Scottish) Infantry Division. He had just learned that his friend, Joe McCulloch, a pre-war footballer with Celtic, had been killed when the tank in which he was travelling was hit. Ward, in peacetime a professional footballer with Derby County, was distraught. In 1940, he had played with McCulloch for the Scottish Army at Ibrox Stadium in Glasgow and had served with him, and played with him, since.

When he rejoined his unit at Uelzen, Germany, at a camp near the River Elbe, he found himself dressing the wounds of captured German soldiers. Then the unit was taken to a place 10 miles (16km) north of Celle in Lower Saxony. And, for all the death and destruction that he had seen so far, Ward was utterly unprepared for the sights that confronted him. Men, women and children were dying at the rate of 500 a day and, among thousands of typhus-infected corpses, thousands more lay seriously ill. Ward had seen plenty of death and destruction on his way here from the Normandy beach where he had staggered ashore, seasick, ten months earlier. But this was inhumanity on an industrial scale. Cruelty, squalor, degradation, disease. The piles of human bones were knee-deep. More than 60,000 starving and terminally sick people had been left with no food, water or sanitation.

British tanks arrived with flame-throwers to burn the rotting corpses. On this warm spring day, Ward and his colleagues looked on in disbelief. What was this place?

It was Bergen-Belsen. Belsen for short. It was a concentration camp.

Belsen had been liberated by the British Second Army on 15 April 1945. Richard Dimbleby was the first broadcaster to report on that day. His ten-minute radio piece was so shocking that, at first, the BBC would not play it. Indeed, at first, they could not believe such a harrowing account of the nightmare in which Dimbleby had found himself. In one passage he said, 'One woman, distraught to the point of madness, flung herself at a British soldier who was on guard in the camp on the night that it was reached by the 11th Armoured Division. She begged him to give her some milk for the tiny baby she held in her arms. She laid the mite on the ground, threw herself at the sentry's feet and kissed his boots. And when in his distress he asked her to get up, she put the baby in his arms and ran off crying that she would find milk for it because there was no milk in her breast. And when the soldier opened the bundle of rags to look at the child, he found it had been dead for days. I have never seen British soldiers so moved to cold fury as the men who opened the Belsen camp this week.'

Daily News journalist Colin Wills told a similar story:

'In huge enclosures about me were 60,000 men and women of many nations, including allied prisoners of war, German political prisoners and German criminals, all of them starving ... the day before yesterday [German SS guards] added to the hideous charnel by shooting many prisoners ... I have not checked the figures yet, but the bullet-riddled bodies are there ...

'The prisoners have had a kilo and a half (3lbs 3oz) of bread and two bowls of watery soup daily. When the camp was overrun, they raided the cookhouse, ate what food was there, and then raided the filthy swill bins and ate the offal ...

'British loudspeaker vans are broadcasting in six languages, explaining what is being done for them. They are wandering about in thousands, men and women, all dressed in striped suits once blue and white but now indescribably filthy.

'Today I met a man from Ramsgate who had escaped when the Germans moved some prisoners from Stalag 357. He spoke of the privations when Red Cross parcels did not arrive. "But that," he said, "was heaven compared with what the Russians suffered. We saw Russians starved to death. We managed to smuggle them some of our Red Cross parcels. Sometimes they were so weak that they could not thank us or stand up to shake hands. They would crawl forward and kiss our feet."'

Reuters special correspondent Doon Campbell described what he had seen at Belsen: 'In one hut I found about fifty men huddled almost sore-to-sore. One seemed to have a rail over his head. Then you recognised his arms. One seemed just bone until you went close to him and saw that he had skin as well. One was trying to stand on stringlike legs that dangled from a torso the thickness of a naval hawser. But they all said, "Hello," and tried to smile. Half these men were professors, inventors, intellectuals, industrialists ...' Major J.P. Fox of the Royal Army Medical Corps told Campbell, 'The camp may have started off as properly as any concentration camp could be started, but it degenerated until it existed solely for the amusement of the SS.'

War correspondent John D'Arcy-Dawson told how he had 'risked typhus to get this story so that readers of the *Daily Record* can know to what depths of degradation Nazism leads mankind'.

'The Nazi SS guards in spotless uniforms, well fed and strong, were still on guard pending the arrival of our troops. These Nazis laughed and joked as they stood around with their machine-guns, and they laughed at a typical Nazi joke, for last night they massacred hundreds of starving prisoners because they raided a field of rotten potatoes, putrid and black. ... Coming from the filthy kitchen out into the sunlight, I stepped over the dead lying unburied with their fingers still clawing for the potatoes. These were some of the hundreds shot dead last night by these same Nazi guards that I had passed. I walked down the compound past recumbent forms. I could not tell the dead from the living, so still were they. Around them, children played noisily, for death has no horrors in this camp where thousands die every day from starvation. Walking through the compounds we were followed by the prisoners who pressed upon us their lice-ridden bodies. We could not stop them, and when some poor, filthy remnant of humanity held out his hand in gratefulness for our coming, we could not refuse to take that shrunken talon once strong with the vigour of youth.'

On 13 April 1945, the *Newcastle Evening Chronicle* told its readers that if felt it its duty to publish 'another terrible story of German atrocities ... so that the beastliness we're fighting can be fully understood'.

Lawrence Fairhall, the *Evening Chronicle*'s war correspondent, reported from Gardelgan concentration camp in Northern Germany:

'Charred and fused remains of 700 Russians, Poles and Hungarians still lie here this morning midst the smouldering and burning wreckage of a once straw-filled barn into which they had been herded and burnt to death by German SS troops recently recruited from the Hitler Youth. Even now, five days after they had met their terrible end, the smell of death fills the air as US Army investigators, carefully moving some of their still burning bodies and charred remains, gather evidence of this most frightful German atrocity to be unearthed on the Western Front.

Hard, bitter American fighting men have vomited at the sights which have befallen their eyes. This is not just another atrocity story but cold, facts welded into a terrible indictment to be charged against the German nation as a whole for condoning such crimes committed in their name ... It is worth remembering that this atrocity occurred only last Friday while the Allied armies were still sweeping across the face of Germany.'

On 20 April, the British Army Film and Photographic Unit asked General Sir Miles Dempsey, commander of the British Second Army, to recommend the extension of the visit of ten members of the House of Commons and House of Lords to Belsen, 'where Army men accustomed to blood and death have been shocked what they have seen'. 'They wanted all the British people to know what the Germans have done.'

Belsen had first been established as a prisoner-of-war camp in 1940. In 1943, Jewish civilians who held foreign passports were held here in the hope that they could be exchanged for German nationals held by the Allies. But then Belsen was used as a collection centre for those who had managed to survive the forced marches – the 'death marches' – when other camps were evacuated in the face of the Soviet offensive in the east. The Nazis did not want this secret to be out.

As the Allies advanced into the heart of Germany and beyond, tens of thousands of other concentration camp victims were liberated, although thousands still died later, their condition far too bad for them to be saved. The names of those camps joined Bergen-Belsen in the catalogue of infamy. They included the huge Auschwitz-Birkenau complex in Occupied Poland; Dachau in Bavaria, the first concentration camp to be opened by the Nazis, as long ago as 1933; Buchenwald, opened in 1937, where, as well as Jewish people, Communists and other political prisoners, Romas, Jehovah's Witnesses, Freemasons, mentally ill and physically disabled people, 'sexual deviants' and ordinary criminals met their end. Its Ohrdruf sub-camp was the first to be liberated by US troops. Also Ravensbrück, 56 miles (90km) north of Berlin, which was exclusively for female prisoners; Mauthausen, 12 miles (19.3km) east of Linz in Austria, the main camp of almost 100 sub-camps; Sachsenhausen-Oranienburg in Germany, where Joseph Stalin's eldest son was a prisoner. The list goes on and on. Six camps were dedicated to extermination, but hundreds of thousands of people were tortured and murdered elsewhere too. More than 1.3 million, around 85 per cent of those sent there, were killed at Auschwitz-Birkenau alone. Altogether, some six million Jewish people, and between half a million and five million others (the figure for the 'others' is disputed and can never be proved), were systematically murdered across occupied Europe, in gas chambers, gas vans, mass shootings, or just simply starved and worked to death by the Nazis.

The 28 April 1945 edition of the *Illustrated London News* included a four-page photographic supplement that contained images of Belsen and the Mittelbau-Dora (near Nordhausen in Thuringia) concentration camps: 'Nothing that Dante could conceive of the Inferno we term Hell can exceed in agony the ghastly scenes.' The magazine told its readers, 'Our subscribers with young families, whom they should not desire to see the photographs, can remove these pages, which are easily detachable by sharp pull, from the remainder of our issue.'

In April 1945, *Daily News* reporter Norman Clark was in Weimar:

'The Germans you meet – often in the village where a concentration camp is sited – scoff unbelievingly when you ask them about the atrocities committed in their midst and in their name. These are the distortions of propaganda they will tell you, or else they try to dismiss the subject by conceding that there may have been one or two cases, but there must have been good reasons for them. They protest that the German nation cannot be held responsible, that no German would be capable of committing them.'

The locals, however, were not being allowed to forget or to disbelieve, said Clark. They were being taken to the camps to view for themselves the corpses of unburied prisoners, and to see those starving, themselves so close to death.

'A thousand citizens of Weimar went to Buchenwald today, walking 6 miles (9.6k) through the leafy forest which they knew as a spot for picnics. In groups of 100 they made the tour of the camp. In the crematorium they saw the blackened skeletons and skulls in the ovens; in the yard outside the heap of white human ashes and bones, and a tumbril piled high with the naked bodies of inmates who had died in the camp that night and awaited burial. They were escorted wherever they went by MPs and walked about the camp stared upon by the inmates, ragged clothes on emaciated bodies.

'Women in the parties cried; men, including uniformed German policemen, were white-faced and looked shocked ... Some of the men in the parties broke down towards the end of the inspection, and several women who fainted could be taken no further. They filed through the long huts where the scrawny bodies of inmates too ill or weak to rise lay on the bare boards of the three-tier line of bunks, one blanket covering three frames.

'In the riding stables, where Thälmann, the German Communist leader, and unnumbered hundreds of others were shot, they saw the hooks and nooses by which hundreds more were hanged. They walked through the research laboratories where doctors experimented with new serums, using human beings as pathological guinea pigs with fatal results in 90 per cent of the cases. What the Germans saw they will never be able to forget, as anyone else who has visited the camp can vouch.'

The Scotsman commented,

'As the Allies advance into Germany, the truth about German concentration camps is being revealed in all its stark horror. It was, of course, known that such camps existed. The names of Dachau near Munich, Oranienburg near Berlin, Duerrgoy near Breslau, and Boergermoor in north-west Germany, were symbols for the torture and murder which the Nazi State authorised and applied first to Jews ... No doubt it is a painful and terrible experience for German citizens to be marched through these camps of torture and death, but it is right that Germans should see, with their own eyes, horrors the existence of which they would be prone to deny or ignore in after years. There will at least be people in Weimar who will know that the accounts given of the Buchenwald camp are not Allied atrocity stories or Jewish fictions. No doubt the Germans would not know in detail what was happening to many of these prisoners, but they were not so ignorant as not to know in general what went on. They accepted the system perhaps with a shrug of the shoulders. They were not going to make martyrs of themselves for some abstract principle of freedom. In any case, those who suffered were mainly Jews and foreigners. There is no doubt that the German people found it advisable to shut their eyes to the facts. Because of their moral cowardice they cannot be trusted to put matters right.'

It was not enough, said *The Scotsman*, to organise for German citizens tours round concentration camps. The lasting problem was what to do with a people so lacking in backbone that such a system had been allowed to grow. Education was no remedy. Until 1933 at least, Germany was one of the best-educated countries in the world. It was impossible to give people political sense, 'and the Germans do not seem to have it'. Even if there was a change of heart in Germany, said the newspaper, it would be long years before the stain of the concentration camps could be wiped away.

In May 1945, Tim Ward's unit found themselves at the seaside town of Travermunde on the Baltic coast, as far removed from the horrors of Belsen as could be imagined. One day, when Tim was making one of his routine checks at a nearby hospital, a blond, blue-eyed, upright, undisputedly Aryan boy, aged about 14, appeared. He was wearing shorts and a shirt, and Tim could smell burning. He asked around and discovered that the boy had come down dressed in his Hitler Youth uniform and had slapped his younger brother for queuing with British soldiers. Two of them had ripped the uniform off Wilhelm – for that was his name – and burnt it. Throughout his war, Tim had carried in his ambulance a football, donated by Derby County. He was kicking it around on the beach at Travermunde when he noticed Wilhelm watching from behind a tree. Tim called across: 'Fussball speilen?' The boy suddenly looked less stern. He came over and played with Tim and his pals every day until they moved on.

Chapter 19

Final Curtain

Hitler is reported to be dead … Was there ever such news? Was there ever such a triumph? How can we rejoice enough at the triumph of our men in arms?
Daily Express

'Sewers blocked with corpses, tree-lined avenues ablaze from end to end, pigeons flying with flames singeing their feathers – this is the picture of Berlin given to me by men who have watched the death agony of Hitler's once proud capital. The last desperate resistance is rapidly being beaten down. The battle will soon be over. Berlin is a city of the dead. Bodies of Germans litter the streets. They are entombed in the tunnels of the underground railway system … Everywhere fires are burning fiercely and are likely to burn for days. The Spree river and other waterways are choked with debris and corpses, making it almost impossible for a suction pump to operate.'

So, on 29 April 1945, Reuters special correspondent Duncan Hooper described 'the last blazing hours' of the capital of the Third Reich.

Soviet forces had entered Berlin on 21 April, five days after the beginning of their final offensive in which they had initially tried to encircle the German capital. The Western Allies had called a halt to their aerial bombardment, but the Soviets continued to pound the city from the air as well as firing almost two million artillery shells in support of their ground forces. Soviet troops had first crossed into German territory in October, Joseph Stalin desperate to be the first to reach Berlin. President Roosevelt was happy to let him do so. Roosevelt's eyes were on ending the war against Japan. He wanted the Soviet Union as an ally in that endeavour. Stalin would also be a vital partner in the creation of stable post-war world. For now, he could have Berlin. And, in fierce hand-to-hand fighting against the remnants of the German defenders – SS, Wehrmacht and militia, but also Hitler Youth, some of them no older than 14 – soldiers of the Red Army closed in on Adolf Hitler himself.

Elsewhere, there was other important war news. On 30 April, the *Daily Record* was one of the newspapers that reported the death of Italian dictator Benito Mussolini:

'… the founder of Fascism has been executed. As the bells of liberation rang throughout the city of Milan yesterday, Allied troops pushing into Loreto square saw the suspended bodies of the ex-Duce and seventeen Fascist cabinet members. All had been shot in the back by a partisan firing squad. The executions, which followed a speedy trial before a People's Court, took place in Como, where the bodies were also publicly displayed before removal to Milan … A Swiss eyewitness declared that as the 5th Army spearheads thrust forward to the heart of Milan, they came to a gruesome horrible site …'

On 25 April, Mussolini, wearing a Luftwaffe uniform, together with his 33-year-old mistress, Clara Pettaci, had been heading for the Swiss border when they were recognised by partisans and taken to the small town of Giulino de Mezzegra on the shores of Lake Como. There they were executed by machine-gun fire before their bodies, together with those of fourteen fellow Fascists, were dumped in a van and taken to Milan to be put on show in the Piazzale Loreto, where, eight months earlier, had been displayed the bodies of fifteen executed partisans. Before they were hung upside down from a metal girder on the half-built Standard Oil service station, the corpses were abused by an angry crowd that pelted them with vegetables, kicked them and fired guns at them. The *New York Times* called it 'a fitting end to a wretched life'.

So, Mussolini was dead, Italy was all but completely liberated, the Soviets were in Berlin, and there were reports that the Nazi surrender of Germany was imminent. Details, though, were muddled. American radio and newspaper correspondents put out a story that Heinrich Himmler was the man offering to give up the fight. But, according to Martin Agronsky, Washington correspondent of the Blue Radio network, the surrender offer was not made by Himmler or Hitler, but by the German High Command, 'a group of people considered by high officials in London, Washington and Moscow as competent enough to surrender the German Armies to the Allies'.

A 'high British source' in San Francisco had told the British United Press agency that Himmler had sent word through Stockholm that Hitler 'may not live another twenty-four hours'. Reuters added that Hitler was a very sick man who would not last forty-eight hours after any announcement of an unconditional surrender. Such a shock would cause his death.

Rumours swept through the world's capitals. Travellers arriving in Switzerland from Germany claimed that, along with Goering and Goebbels, Hitler had already been killed.

Moscow Radio reported that Hitler and Goebbels had fled Berlin and were hiding in the Austrian Tyrol: 'Hitler held a meeting with Nazi chiefs in the new seat of his command. He got to this meeting by plane from the Tyrol. It was established at this meeting that the German High Command had lost control of communications with separate fighting units, and orders were given that commanders should act on their own initiative. After this meeting, Hitler hastily returned to the Tyrol.' Oslo Radio had it that Hitler was still in Berlin, directing its defence.

So many conflicting reports, but what was clear, according to the diplomatic correspondent of *The People*, was that 'the Third Reich, planned by Hitler to endure for a thousand years, is toppling now on the abyss of final destruction'.

'It is going to its doom in a welter of rumoured revolution, of total surrender feelers and of reported assassinations of the men who led it through years of battle to its melodramatic end. The world last night waited expectantly and tensely for the end as message after message flashing over cables and wireless waves pointed to the swift and complete dissolution of the remnants of the shattered Nazi empire.'

In Munich, birthplace of the Nazi Party, the city's radio reported that General Ritter von Epp, the 76-year-old state commissioner for Bavaria, had said that he intended to 'break off the fight which had become senseless'. The radio declared that the 'free Bavarian movement' had seized control of the government at Munich, exhorted the Wehrmacht to lay down their arms and told French prisoners held in labour camps to down tools and walk away. Then a Nazi official took the microphone, branded the broadcast a fake, 'the work of criminals and traitors'. Another report 'from a neutral source' said that Munich had been declared an open city by the German Army. Units of the American Third Army, who were only 25 miles (40km) from Munich, picked up Epp's broadcast in which he asked that Allied aircraft should bomb the headquarters of Field Marshall Albert Kesselring, 6 miles (9.6km) south of the Bavarian capital. The previous month, Kesselring, a Hitler loyalist to the end, had replaced Gerd von Rundstedt as the German Army's commander-in-chief west.

Hitler had held his final war conference on 22 April, once more flying into a rage and then becoming suicidal. Now aged 56, he was still suffering from the effects of the July bomb. His hands shook and he walked with a stumbling gait. His face was grey, and his eyes gave away his state of fatigue. Saliva dribbled from the corner of his mouth, and even on a short walk he was forced to sit and rest. Since 1938, he had been treated by Dr Theo Morrell, who favoured unconventional methods. Hitler soon became a disciple, ignoring the advice of his main physician, Karl Brandt, who warned him against the large doses of drugs and vitamins that Morrell prescribed. When Hitler complained of headaches, stomach cramps or any other ailments, Morrell was there with his injections and pills. It was reported that Hitler was eventually taking up to thirty different kinds of drugs – narcotics to make him sleep, stimulants to keep him awake. Prescription drugs and quack remedies – when Morrell offered them, he swallowed them all. Albert Speer, Hitler's chief architect turned Minister of Armaments and War Production, said that 'one of Morrell's talents was his ability to exaggerate immoderately any illness he cured in order to cast his skill in the proper light'.

By April 1945, the Nazi leader's moods were lurching between wild anger and black despair. He ranted on. Without him, Germany was lost. He had been deserted by his friends, his generals were no more than rats leaving a sinking ship, there was no-one to succeed him. Hess had gone mad, Himmler would be rejected by the Nazi Party and Goering had lost the sympathy of the German people.

Then, on 23 April 1945, Martin Bormann handed Hitler a telegram from Goering, who was now almost 500 miles (804km) away in the Bavarian Alps:

'My Führer:
General Koller today gave me a briefing on the basis of communications given to him by Colonel General Jodl and General Christian, according to which you had referred certain decisions to me and emphasised that I, in case negotiations would become necessary, would be in an easier position than you in Berlin. These views were so surprising and serious to me that I felt obligated to assume, in case by 2200 hours no answer is forthcoming, that you have lost your freedom of action. I shall then view the conditions of your decree as fulfilled and take action for the well-being of Nation and Fatherland. You know what I feel for you in these most difficult hours of my life, and I cannot express this in words. God protect you and allow you despite everything to come here as soon as possible.
   Your faithful Hermann Goering'

In essence, Goering was simply asking if he should assume leadership of the Third Reich in the event of Hitler remaining in the Führerbunker, unable to govern. Bormann, the head of the Nazi Party Chancellery and effectively Hitler's private secretary, wielded immense power. He offered the view that Goering was attempting a coup d'etat. Then another message arrived from Goering, this time addressed to the Reichminister of Foreign Affairs, Joachim von Ribbentrop:

'I have asked the Führer to provide me with instructions by 10pm, April 23. If by this time it is apparent that the Führer *has* been deprived of his freedom of action to conduct the affairs of the Reich, his decree of June 29, 1941, becomes effective, according to which I am heir to all his offices as his deputy. [If] by 12 midnight April 23, 1945, you receive no other word either from the Führer *directly* or from me, you are to come to me at once by air.'

It was more ammunition for Bormann. Goering, he said, was announcing that, by midnight, he would take office as leader of the Third Reich. If a weary Hitler had been unmoved by Goering's first message, his second prompted an immediate reaction. He stripped Goering of all rights of succession, accused him of treason but said that he would be spared further punishment if he resigned all his offices on health reasons. It was Bormann who drafted that message to Goering, while Hitler sunk back into the sullen mood that had gripped him for most of that day. According to *Inside The Third Reich,* the autobiography of Albert Speer, written while he was serving a twenty-year prison sentence following his trial at Nuremberg, Hitler said, 'Well, all right. Let Goering negotiate the surrender. If the war is lost anyhow, it doesn't matter who does it.'

On 29 April 1945, as members of the Hitler Youth faced Russian artillery in Berlin, Hitler made final arrangements. He left all but his art collection – that was meant for his home town of Braunau – to the Nazi Party, and he named Admiral Karl Doenitz as his successor as ruler of the Third Reich. Then he married his long-time partner, Eva Braun, the 33-year-old former employee of his personal photographer, Heinrich Hoffman. Braun had been kept firmly in the background throughout their relationship. She had made her way to the Führerbunker on 15 April, saying that she would remain with Hitler until the end. For showing such loyalty to him, Hitler decided that, at last, she should be his wife. Albert Speer later wrote, '… everyone in the bunker knew why she had come. Figuratively and in reality, with her presence a messenger of death moved into the bunker'.

On 30 April, Hitler had his beloved Alsatian dog, Blondi, put down. Then he said goodbye to his closest staff before going back to his own rooms. It was mid-afternoon. His bodyguard, Rochus Misch, recalled, 'Everyone was waiting for the shot. We were expecting it … Then came the shot. Heinz Linge [an SS officer and Hitler's valet] took me to one side and we went in. I saw Hitler slumped by the table. I didn't see any blood on his head [other accounts described Hitler's head as 'shattered' and a bloodstained carpet]. And I saw Eva with her knees drawn up lying next to him on the sofa –

wearing a white and blue blouse, with a little collar: just a little thing.' She had swallowed cyanide.

Linge's account differed. No sound was heard from the room, and it was ten minutes, and only after the pungent smell of a discharged firearm, before they entered. 'Everything in me resisted opening the door,' he wrote later.

Now what to do with the bodies? Hitler had ordered SS officer Otto Günsche to cremate his remains. He did not want his body to go on show like that of Mussolini. Soaked in petrol, the corpses of Adolf Hitler and Eva Braun were set alight. They burned into the evening before the remains were buried in what passed for a garden at the bunker. Soviet troops later found part of a lower jawbone and two dental bridges, and dental technicians later identified the bone as belonging to Hitler and the bridges as Eva Braun's.

The *Sunday Mirror* for 29 April 1945 had carried a gruesome photograph of two dead children and their mother:

> 'Today the German people are learning that they must pay the price for their trust in Hitler. This woman has paid. When our soldiers captured Schweinfurt, they found her dead. She had poisoned herself and her children rather than face the future in a country ravaged and defeated by war that had already taken her husband, killed in the fighting for the town. Retribution is coming swiftly to the German nation. It is not to be measured in terms of its dead on the battlefield. For the women and children who are left know that they cannot escape their responsibilities for the awful crimes of Belsen and Buchenwald. Those who suffered the oppression in their own lives welcome their conquerors; the rest see only the grave as a way out of their miseries.'

The Führerbunker had not seen its last horror, either. The day following Hitler's death, the six children of Joseph Goebbels – Helga, 12, Hildegard, 11, Helmut, 9, Holdine, 8, Hedwig, 6, and Heidrun, 4 – were all killed. Most accounts have them injected with morphine before a cyanide pill was crushed into each of their mouths. Bruises found on Helga's body led to speculation that she had struggled. Then Goebbels and his wife, Magda, took their own lives. Again, accounts of how they died vary.

Outside of the bunker, the debate over whether Hitler really was dead continued. Reuters reported that, according to reports, at noon the previous day 'in the subterranean HQ of the Nazis in the Tiergarten in Berlin', Adolf Hitler had died, either killed, or by suicide or as the result of a stroke. The *Daily Record*'s front page carried the hopeful headline, 'The War in Europe May Come To An End in A Few Days' Time'.

Hitler's death was announced by Admiral Doenitz over German radio on 1 May, but the situation remained unclear. Newspapers were full of the horror story of the liberation of Belsen concentration camp, and reports of Hitler's death were still unsubstantiated. 'Hitler may be lying dead in Berlin or be cowering in Berchtesgaden,' said Brigadier Edgar Carnegie Anstey, DSO, the military correspondent of the *Daily Dispatch*. Hamburg radio reported that, at 9pm the previous day, Hitler had awarded the Knight's Cross of the Iron Cross to four members of the Wehrmacht. At the same time as the Hamburg broadcast, German-controlled Oslo Radio was interrupted by a voice breaking in several times to say, 'What are you fighting for now? Your Führer is already dead.'

'Hitler: Alive or Dead?' the *Nottingham Journal* wanted to know. Moscow Radio suggested that an announcement of Hitler's death might just be a ruse to prepare for Hitler the possibility of disappearing 'underground': 'The Nazis are unable to give any details about Hitler's death in the Chancellery, for the very simple reason that he was not there at all, neither on 1 May, nor many days, or even weeks, previous to that day. If Hitler is dead, he did not die in Berlin, and he did not die yesterday. There is every reason to believe that he is not dead at all.' Then William Forrest, the *News Chronicle*'s war correspondent embedded with the US Ninth Army, reported that Russian officers at Wittenberg had told him that Hitler was definitely dead. 'He was killed by our troops in the Berlin battle,' they told him.

The *Daily Herald* decided to publish Hitler's obituary, anyway. Written by Norman Ewer, it was entitled, 'The Slum Dweller Who Tried to Make the World a Slum'. Hitler's end, said Ewer, was a 'fitting close' to a 'strange and evil pilgrimage'.

The final days of Berlin as the capital of Hitler's 'thousand-year Reich' were a time of unspeakable horrors for civilians. There were thousands of accounts of the most dreadful atrocities, and it is estimated that hundreds of thousands – maybe as many as two million throughout Germany in the final six months of the war – were raped by Red Army soldiers. Some German soldiers managed to flee to the west, to surrender to British and American forces rather than be captured by Russians. Most did not escape. Estimates of German casualties vary wildly and are open to debate. The Soviets claimed more than 450,000 killed and almost 480,000 captured. German figures give between 92,000 and 100,000 dead. It is estimated that up to 125,000 civilians were also killed. The battle for Berlin had cost the Soviets more than 80,000 killed or missing, and more than a quarter of a million wounded.

On 2 May, the commander of the Berlin defence area, General Helmuth Weidling, called upon his troops to surrender. Hitler's suicide, he told them, meant that he had abandoned them:

'According to the Führer's order, you German soldiers would have had to go on fighting for Berlin despite the fact that our ammunition has run out and despite the general situation which makes our further resistance meaningless. I order the immediate cessation of resistance. Every hour you keep on fighting prolongs the suffering of the civilians in Berlin and of our wounded. Together with the commander-in-chief of the Soviet forces I order you to stop fighting immediately.'

Karl Doenitz authorised General Alfred Jodl to sign an unconditional surrender of all German forces. At 2.41am on 7 May 1945, at Eisenhower's headquarters at Reims in North-Eastern France, Jodl put his name to the Act of Military Surrender, which was witnessed by General Walter Smith on behalf of Eisenhower, by Major General Ivan Susloparov on behalf of the Soviet High Command and Major General François Sevez of the French Army. Eisenhower had refused to meet with the Germans until the surrender had been accomplished.

There were still difficulties, however. The Soviet chief of staff, General Alexei Antonov, expressed concern that the continued fighting in the east between Germany and the Soviet Union made the Reims surrender look like a separate peace. Stalin, meanwhile, was also unhappy about a document signed by Hitler's nominated successor. It could be legitimate only if it was signed by Field Marshal Wilhelm Keitel, the supreme commander of all German forces. On 8 May, in the Berlin suburb of Karlshorst, Keitel obliged, and the German surrender, with few significant changes from the one signed at Reims, was thus ratified by all the Allies. The people of Britain, meanwhile, were ready to celebrate VE Day.

Chapter 20

On This Great Day …

In this hour of victory the city bore her scars with enhanced dignity … it was the price of sacrifice and service; it was a price which history will record as inspiration to future generations … behind the singing and dancing, the colourful display of bunting and the national favours, one sensed something infinitely deeper. It was the sanctuary of the heart.

Western Morning News

In the late spring of 1945, as it became clear that the war in Europe was almost over, attention turned to how the nation would celebrate. It did not help that no-one could predict when what had been known informally as 'V-Day' until the Government opted for 'VE Day' – Victory in Europe Day, to reinforce the idea of a job only partly done – would be.

There was confusion among the population, and concern in Government circles that national chaos might ensue should, the instant victory was declared, everyone simply down tools. With this in mind, business owners were advised to display posters informing staff and customers of their plans for VE Day and VE Plus-One Day well in advance. Mass shop closures and a sudden halt to the supply chain could, without warning, leave families without food for several days.

To that end, on 1 May, most newspapers carried the following advice from the Ministry of Food: 'Grocers should remain open on VE Day for at least one hour, and if possible for two hours, after the announcement has been made. If VE Day should come on a Friday, grocers are asked to open Saturday and close on Monday. Dairymen must deliver milk both on VE Day and VE Plus-One Day. Restaurants are asked to keep open on those days. Wherever practicable, bakers are asked to keep open for an hour, or if necessary two hours, after the announcement, and open on VE Plus-One Day for an hour or two for the sale of bread only. Shops dealing in perishable food, such as fish, vegetables and, where sufficient storage is not available, meat, should keep open for a sufficient time after the announcement to clear stocks. Wholesalers in general will close on the two days.' It was also announced that 'a small supply of Australian currants' would be released for sale at a ration-book points value of sixteen per lb.

The following day, advice was given regarding theatres, music halls, cinemas and public dancing venues: 'The Government think that these might be allowed to remain open later than the normal closing hour.' It was also hoped that local authorities 'will be able to make arrangements for local festivities in their parks and open spaces' and suggested that applications for 'special orders of exemption or special permission for an extension of the evening permitted hours on VE Day should receive sympathetic consideration'.

It was also revealed that 'there will be no objection to bonfires, but the Government trust that the paramount necessity of ensuring that only material with no salvage value is used and that the desirability of proper arrangements with the National Fire Service to guard against any possible spread of the fire will be borne in mind by those arranging bonfires'. With the continuing fuel shortage, street lighting was not to be returned to normal but, for one night only, those towns and cities not on the coast, where blackout and dim-out restrictions remained, were to be permitted to use floodlighting.

The long wait for VE Day to finally be declared tested the patience of the most ardent patriot and, although the ceasefire had been announced the previous day, the morning of 8 May 1945 began like any other wartime Tuesday.

At 11am at Buckingham Palace, the Changing of the Guard saw the khaki-clad Irish Guards mount the new palace guard. A rainy morning was giving way to broken sunshine as crowds, anticipating an official announcement of peace in Europe, gathered outside and, as at least one newspaper would describe, 'like ants on the base of the Victoria memorial'.

Inside, the king was at work in the ballroom holding an investiture for more than 270 military and civil defence personnel. After presenting a number of George Medals, Military Medals and Distinguished Service Medals, the king entertained Winston Churchill over lunch before the prime minister returned to 10 Downing Street to make his victory speech at 3pm. A little more than ten minutes later, King George VI, Queen Elizabeth, Princess Elizabeth and Princess Margaret Rose stepped out onto the palace balcony. Ever since they had seen Churchill's car leave the palace, the crowd had been chanting 'We Want The King!'. Now their monarch, and his family, joined in the celebrations while, high above them, a huge Royal Standard fluttered gently. Throughout the afternoon and into the evening, an estimated 100,000 people gathered in front of the palace and were rewarded by several more balcony appearances. At 5.30pm, to the delight of the crowd, the royal family were joined by the prime minister, who had been invited back to the palace, along with members of the War Cabinet, for a formal audience in the Bow Room. And there was another appearance just before 9pm. Then the king made another broadcast to the Empire. The speech, which lasted more than ten minutes, began thus:

'Today we give thanks to Almighty God for a great deliverance. Speaking from our Empire's oldest capital city, war-battered but never for one moment daunted or dismayed – speaking from London, I ask you to join with me in that act of thanksgiving ... at this hour, when the dreadful shadow of war has passed from our hearths and homes in these islands, we may at last make one pause for thanksgiving and then turn our thoughts to the tasks all over the world which peace in Europe brings with it.'

The monarch spoke of the war dead and noted the efforts of all: 'Armed or unarmed, men and women, you have fought, striven, and endured to your utmost. No-one knows that better than I do; and as your King I thank with a full heart those who bore arms so valiantly on land and sea, or in the air; and all civilians who, shouldering their many burdens, have carried them unflinchingly without complaint ... everything was at stake: our freedom, our independence, our very existence as a people ... we were defending the liberties of the whole world ... we knew that, if we failed, the last remaining barrier against a worldwide tyranny would have fallen in ruins.'

Now he called upon the people to continue their efforts: 'Much hard work awaits us, both in the restoration of our own country after the ravages of war and in helping to restore peace and sanity to a shattered world. This comes upon us at a time when we have all given of our best. For five long years and more, heart and brain, nerve and muscle have been directed upon the overthrow of Nazi tyranny. Now we turn, fortified by success, to deal with our last remaining foe ... together we shall all face the future with stern resolve and prove that our reserves of willpower and vitality are inexhaustible ... let us turn our thoughts on this day of just triumph and proud sorrow; and then take up our work again, resolved as a people to do nothing unworthy of those who died for us and to make the world such a world as they would have desired, for their children and for ours. This is the task to which now honour binds us.'

The king and his family then stepped out onto the balcony again. At around 10.45pm, as the crowds continued to party, a group of a dozen or so friends slipped out of what one of the group – Jean Woodroffe – called 'one of the backdoors of Buckingham Palace' to celebrate with the people. Among them were Princesses Elizabeth and Margaret Rose, with the blessing of their parents, although under the watchful eyes of accompanying equerry Peter Townsend and other officers.

In February 1944, to help with his official duties, the king had appointed Wing Commander Peter Townsend DSO and DFC and Bar, a man who, during the 1930s, had been the future monarch's flight instructor and was a Battle of Britain pilot. In February 1940, Townsend had been one of the three

Hurricane pilots who had combined to shoot down a Luftwaffe Heinkel 111 north of Whitby – the first enemy aircraft to crash on English soil during the war. While with No. 85 Squadron, Townsend had been forced to ditch in the Channel, and, just a month later, was shot down over Tonbridge, suffering a wound that would eventually necessitate the amputation of a big toe. He received a Bar to his DFC in September 1940 for leading his squadron as it protected convoys. Four of the ten enemy aircraft the squadron shot down were credited to Townsend. Almost a decade later, Townsend's romance with Princess Margaret would become the subject of headline-making public gossip.

Now, however, he was simply one of several keeping a watchful eye on the two young princesses as they mingled with the joyous throng. According to one of the party – 'Porchey', later to become the 7th Earl of Carnarvon – they moved freely and entirely unrecognised around central London. Margaret Rhodes, the princesses' cousin, later said that, at around 11.30pm, the group arrived at the Ritz where they did the conga. 'The Ritz has always been so stuffy and formal – we rather electrified the stuffy individuals inside. I don't think people realised who was among the party – I think they thought it was just a group of drunk young people. I remember old ladies looking faintly shocked. As one congaed through, eyebrows were raised.'

They continued through Whitehall, Piccadilly, to Hyde Park Corner and Green Park. Heading back down the Mall, they linked arms and sang. Speaking about the evening some forty years later, Queen Elizabeth II said: 'We were terrified of being recognised – so I pulled my uniform cap well down over my eyes. A Grenadier officer among our party of about sixteen people said he refused to be seen in the company of another officer improperly dressed. So, I had to put my cap on normally … I think it was one of the most memorable nights of my life.'

Margaret Rhodes said, 'There were these masses and masses of people. There was a general thing of "We want the King and Queen", which we all frantically joined in with and were amazed when, five or ten minutes later, the windows opened and they came out on to the balcony, although it seemed that, on this occasion, they might just have received word that their daughters were in the crowd outside. A final balcony appearance came at half past midnight before the palace floodlights were extinguished.'

That evening, two ATS personnel took two mobile anti-aircraft searchlights to St Paul's Cathedral, a miraculous survivor with only minor damage from the Blitz. They switched them on at 10.15pm, later saying, 'This is the day we have been waiting for … this is the pleasantest job we have had.'

Such joyous scenes had been repeated through Britain, although, to put a dampener on the day for which people had waited years, on the morning of

8 May much of Britain had woken to cloudy skies and rain – and, for the first time since 1939, it was not unexpected. Throughout the war, the publishing of weather forecasts had been forbidden for fear of aiding enemy bombers. Now, rather than printing retrospective reports, it was considered safe to let people know that they might need an umbrella.

The *Birmingham Post* reported,

> 'The morning rain made the outlook dismal, and at first there was little to indicate that this was the day for which people had waited for more than five-and-a-half years, except for the bunting, flags, and other decorations with which the city was plentifully decorated. Even these, bedraggled and drooping, seemed almost to mock the occasion. Nevertheless, preparations in the suburbs went on, householders adding the last touches to their decorated windows and houses, and many children, emerging in dresses and suits of red, white and blue, and other pre-war finery.'

As it happened, when the time to celebrate did come,

> the weather was largely incidental, as the *Birmingham Post* of 9 May reported: 'VE Day was celebrated in Birmingham yesterday in a manner that was, in general, in keeping with the occasion. They remembered that this was only a pause and that the final chapter could not be written until the war in the Far East had been won. It was a day of thanksgiving in churches and homes, and of celebrations in the streets, by citizens of a city than which none has made a greater contribution to victory. They recognised their right to rejoice yet did not forget those who could be beside them only in spirit.'

The report was illustrated by a photograph of the crowds celebrating in Victoria Square as well as an advertisement from Lewis's store, which promised its customers and staff, 'Lewis's will open tomorrow, 10 May at 9.30am, following a thanksgiving service for staff.'

Across the country, prayers were being said, remembrances made and glasses raised. The *Western Mail* of 9 May reported that in South Wales 'it was a day of contrasts':

> 'One had the early impression that Cardiff was little too subdued. True, the city was dressed in red, white, and blue, with the "little streets" challenging each other in a display of colour. Everywhere men, women and children wore red, white, and blue rosettes, but it was not until the

memorable service in the civic centre was over that the people really let themselves go. Cathays Park, always majestic, never presented a more inspiring picture. There were between 20,000 and 25,000 people present … thousands of people assembled to pay homage. Flags flew proudly. Sentiment and gaiety marched arm-in-arm.'

Cardiff's Lord Mayor, Alderman Walter Howell Parker, addressed the crowds: 'We have especial cause for thanks when we realise how near we have been to defeat and the terrible consequences it would have entailed. Let us raise our voices in thanksgiving to God for our deliverance and pray that our future shall prove worthy of His Grace.'

The *Western Mail* summed up the mood: 'In Kingsway, American "Dough Boys" and British Jack Tars held an impromptu dance; pretty girls linked arms with strangers. It was all so friendly: five-and-a-half years of war had taught us to be good neighbours. The city throbbed with new life … it was gay, happy and alert, ablaze with merriment.'

Elsewhere in the city, ships' sirens and horns blasted out joyously and detonators were placed on the tram lines so that each time a tram went by it produced explosions and clouds of smoke that enveloped it. A sizeable Moslem community at Cardiff docks spent the day in 'solemn thanksgiving … the majority of the men are seafarers and losses in the Merchant Navy have meant a heavy toll among them'.

The celebrations meant that in Cardiff, as in other towns and cities, scheduled events were cancelled or postponed. The Central Council of Physical Recreation postponed its 8 May Demonstration of Purposeful Physical Training in Industry until the autumn, while Cardiff Technical College postponed all its part-time classes on VE Day and the following two days. Those taking examinations, however, were not excused.

In Swansea, where many of the buildings were 'lavishly decorated', a number of streets hung up their own 'Siegfried lines', some of which were decorated with what the *Western Mail* called 'the more intimate objects of wearing apparel'. Some streets held impromptu outdoor parties. And that morning a drum-head service was held in the forecourt of the Old Guildhall for navy, army, air force and other Allied service personnel stationed at the port.

A group of Llanelli folk took some persuading that hostilities with Germany were at an end. When four German prisoners of war were spotted, some members of the crowd decided to aim fireworks at them. Fortunately, only one proved accurate and the car in which they rode was able to escape.

In Scotland on 1 May, the 'Bats in the Belfry' column by 'the Gangrel' in the *Daily Record* had warned readers,

'Official spokesmen are steadfastly plugging the warning that VE Day should be no occasion for mafficking and whoopee, but rather a solemn pause for renewed stiffening of the upper lip, tightening the belt, elevating the socks, jutting the jaw and clenching the tooth … with the victory announcement expected at 8am we're going to need the last ounce of willpower, sheer grit, intestinal fortitude, sand in the craw and steely resolution to leave that bottle alone until the sun is in proper relation to the yardarm.'

In Glasgow, the Corporation Electricity Department arranged for floodlighting of the façades of large city buildings, such as Glasgow City Chambers, which was also draped in the flags of the Allied nations, and in 'shields and greenery', while coloured fairy lights festooned George Square, and the bells of local churches and the city's famous Tollbooth Steeple rang out.

Unfortunately, some of the preparedness had unintentional consequences. Thanks to the Food Ministry's advice, housewives across Glasgow had bought in an extra loaf of bread for VE Day. But no-one was certain when VE Day would be. Housewives simply had to guess. Predictably, they were guided by what they saw others doing and, on the morning of 5 May, it seemed everyone had joined a bread queue. By lunchtime, there wasn't a single loaf left in a city shop. One shopkeeper told the *Sunday Post*, 'All week bread sales have been terrific, but this morning was murder. Everybody wanted bread. Some customers were buying four and five loaves a time.'

Even shops who had ordered extra in were caught out by the rush. No-one, it seemed, wanted cream cakes or sponges, just bread. Any bread. The paper reported, 'People with a life-long preference for a small brown or a wee rumpy or a large pan went happily home carrying squares and crusties.'

When VE Day finally did arrive, bread, or a lack of it, mattered not one jot. It seemed everyone in Glasgow was determined to get out on the town. Tramcars and buses were jammed, with scarcely an inch of space to move as 'men, women and children went delirious with pent-up VE Night delight'.

It was estimated that a tenth of Glasgow's population gathered in George Square. Revellers wore paper hats, waved streamers and flags, and climbed statues. Even the police joined in and did nothing to stop fellow citizens from climbing statues and air-raid shelters, from which two sailors threw cigarettes to the crowd gathered below. There was singing and dancing, both the traditional reels and modern jitterbugs. In Exchange Square, a Dutch marine climbed onto an equestrian statue from where he thanked the British people, particularly the Scots, for their help for his homeland.

There were similar scenes 40 miles (64km) away in the Scottish capital. At first, though, there was a meeting of the council at the City Chambers, the Lord Provost, John Ireland Falconer, paid tribute both to the endurance of the British people and the parts played by Scottish men and women. There followed a ceremony at the Mercat Cross, in which the Dean of the Thistle read the *76th Psalm*, just as his predecessor had done in the same spot in 1588 in thanksgiving for the defeat of the Spanish Armada. The official ceremonies done, the real celebrations could begin. Thousands of servicemen, factory workers, shop staff and families came out onto the streets of the city. A crowd gathered outside the American Red Cross Service Club where police were deployed to ensure everyone's safety. From the balcony and open windows above them, the crowd were showered with chocolate bars and chewing gum, and a marine up on a balcony conducted the community singing of *Roll Out the Barrel*, *The Yanks Are Coming*, *Tipperary* and *Land of Hope and Glory*, and torn-up paper fluttered down onto the pavement in true American style. At the Register House, another crowd watched as soldiers and sailors climbed the equestrian statue of the Duke of Wellington. One managed to balance on the mane of the horse, from where he attempted to catch caps thrown up to him – remarkably, he caught quite a few and tried on several of them.

In Montrose, the effect of having to wait for so many days for the Victory in Europe announcement had a clear effect on celebrations. Although flags and bunting had been hung over the High Street, and crowds did gather there, they did so almost silently. A combination of continuing rain and the knowledge that the dim-out was to continue, and that floodlighting and bonfires were still banned, seemed to have a depressing effect. By contrast, in Dumfries, neither the lack of certainty nor the weather prevented people from celebrating. Even if, thanks to changes to the Home Office's anticipated timings, there were fewer people in the streets to hear the official announcement, which was broadcast by way of loudspeakers. The *Dumfries and Galloway Standard* reported that the Provost's party proceeded through 'streets gay with flags, albeit somewhat dispirited flags, because the rain had been falling steadily for some hours'.

According to the *Belfast Newsletter* of 9 May, the streets of Bangor, Northern Ireland, were 'gaily decorated [and] thronged throughout the day by enthusiastic crowds of people. Joyous peals were rung on church bells, and at the thanksgiving services there were very large congregations. The Town Hall was illuminated at night by multi-coloured lights, the centrepiece in the scheme of decorations being the crown and the letters, "VE".'

In Omagh, there was a 'lavish display' of Union Flags and flags of the Allies. An estimated 2,000 soldiers and Auxiliary Territorial Service (ATS) personnel paraded through the town behind the bands of the Royal Inniskilling Fusiliers and the Royal Ulster Rifles, watched by large crowds. The YMCA provided free meals for soldiers and the urban council donated free cigarettes.

In Armagh, there were more church services, parades and music and, at night, there was an open-air dance, and the courthouse was floodlit with fairy lights. In Portadown, businesses displayed photographs of the king and queen, as well as Allied leaders, in their windows, and flags and streamers brought a very festive air to the town.

In Lisburn, there were 'unparalleled scenes of enthusiasm ... the town was beflagged from end to end. Business premises were decorated, and many were illuminated at night. A loudspeaker system was installed in the centre of the town, by means of which Mr Churchill's victory announcement was relayed to a large assemblage of people. The King's message last evening was similarly transmitted. There were bonfires in many districts of the town.'

According to the *Western Morning News* of 9 May, celebrations in Plymouth were, initially at least, more subdued than those seen at the end of the Great War in 1918:

'The edge had been rather taken off a repetition of those excited scenes by the week or two of expectancy, by the unparalleled dramatic events of the past few days leading to the climax. That climax came yesterday afternoon at three o'clock, when ... in the vicinity of the ruins of the ancient mother church of St Andrew, there came through the loudspeakers the familiar voice of the Prime Minister announcing the end of hostilities in Europe ... From the sturdy tower, which alone had stood foursquare to the storms of war, came the peals which have for centuries marked great occasions, and floating in the summer wind, over the heads of the citizens, in a blaze of colour and glory, were the flags of the Allied nations which had made the occasion possible.'

At St Andrew's Church, bellringers worked throughout the day, and while most were able to celebrate, others had to keep on working: 'It was in a fine traditional spirit of service that the appeal for the maintenance of essential services met with full response.'

Being a naval city, VE Day brought the air of a regatta to Plymouth. Out in Plymouth Sound and Devonport Harbour, small boats and big ships were bedecked in flags. There was a degree of confusion about plans for the following days. Thousands of dockworkers, not realising there was a holiday, turned up for work but returned home when they found the gates locked. Many, but not all, schoolchildren turned up as usual but most of their teachers did too, and schools held impromptu thanksgiving services. Plymouth's hospital wards were decorated, and patients were able to listen to the broadcasts by the prime minister and the king. At the City Hospital, patients were given a special tea and there was entertainment too. It may seem remarkable to us today, but servicemen in hospital were given free cigarettes and a bottle of beer 'for those who could drink'. Wounded servicemen at the Prince of Wales's Hospital received a visit from the Lady Mayoress, while those at Plymouth Royal Naval Hospital enjoyed no special treats, save that of listening to Churchill and the king.

There were thanksgiving services at the Royal Naval Barracks, Devonport, and at RAF Harrowbeer at Yelverton. Flags were flown at the Polish Naval HQ while US forces, who had no special plans, were permitted time off. Loudspeakers were erected on Plymouth Hoe and thousands of revellers gathered there to dance until midnight. At a nearby German prisoner-of-war camp, prisoners listened to Churchill's broadcast, which, it was reported, they met with relief.

Admiral Sir Ralph Leatham, Commander-in-Chief at Plymouth, signalled: 'To general in Plymouth Command: On this day of gladness my first thought is to thank the captains, officers, and ships' companies seagoing ships under my command for their gallant and arduous service now rewarded by the utter defeat of Germany. I thank no less the officers and ratings, including the WRNS [Women's Royal Naval Service], whose hard work ashore has sustained and operated the ships. Both afloat and ashore the great naval tradition of the West Country has been nobly upheld. We have not yet achieved peace, and I know I can count on the same fine spirit and unremitting effort until Japan also is overpowered. You have earned the relaxation of VE Day. My best wishes go with you all into the future.'

Another message paid tribute to the volunteer services:

'On this great day women of the Fire Service, Civil Defence, ARP [Air Raid Precautions] Services, Wardens' Service, WVS [Women's Voluntary Service], men and women in our Dockyard, factories, workshops, transport, and utility services, all have made their contribution. It was, indeed, total war. All have borne sacrifice, hardship, loss, long hours, frustration, petty irritation, blackout restrictions, gas exercises, and everything else with great understanding, fortitude, and courage, and all have given much that was precious. And now has come the reward — an almost incredible victory. A total victory that had been won by the whole people. The deliverance had been so miraculous that we must in all humility feel that it owes something, perhaps everything, to more than human effort and human resolution.'

The Lord Mayor told the children of Plymouth that, although 'their happy home life and time of play had been interrupted by the war, soon we would be able to give them more of the happiness that all children enjoy, and should enjoy, in times of peace'.

The people of Skegness, on the Lincolnshire coast, were joined for their celebrations by sailors from HMS *Royal Arthur*, which was a Royal Navy Shore Establishment for training new recruits. It had been requisitioned by the Admiralty from Butlin's holiday camp. Billy Butlin, who had handed over a number of his holiday camps to the military, had agreed to build several new military camps in exchange for their ownership once peace was restored. Skegness, or more accurately Ingoldmells, however, was his first and he helped local children make the most of VE Day by distributing 5,000 free tickets to his amusement park, while the council gave children free rides on the boating lake. That evening, 700 dancers enjoyed a celebration at the Piazza (Butlin's own ballroom had been converted to an armoury) at which £90 was raised for the Skegness Homecoming Fund.

The following Sunday, a service of thanksgiving was held on Skegness Cricket Ground. Three separate parades had formed up from three parts of town, each made up of a different element of the war effort. One with the military, another with Civil Defence and service volunteers, and the third with youth groups and women police officers. They formed up on the cricket field, with local VIPs and civilians seated to the side. The *Skegness News* reported that even the lack of a band to march behind did not prevent them from making 'a very heartening spectacle'.

If the people of Leeds had been forced inside by the early morning rain, then they more than made up for it in the afternoon of VE Day. Out they came into the streets in their thousands, according to the *Yorkshire Post*: 'clad in mackintoshes, carrying umbrellas and wearing red, white and blue favours on their coats and hats'. Many gathered at Leeds Town Hall. In order to keep as many people as dry as possible, the doors to the Victoria Hall were opened. As it happened, just as the prime minister was about to speak, the heavy rain eased to a light drizzle. *The Yorkshire Post* reported that there was 'intense silence' as the crowd listened in.

'You could have heard a pin drop in the Victoria Hall, but Mr Churchill's ringing finale "Advance Britannia! Long live the cause of freedom! God Save the King!" was the signal for a spontaneous outburst of cheering.'

There followed music provided by the Royal Army Pay Corps, the West Yorkshire Regiment and pipers of the Army Selection Training Unit – 'easily the favourites with the crowd'.

By 4pm, more than 8,000 had gathered for the civic service attended by the Lord Mayor and his wife, the Regional Commissioner, the Town Clerk and other civic dignitaries who sat on a dais decorated with red, white and blue lilac. Unfortunately, the rain returned and, perhaps because of this, or because the prime minister had simply said all that needed to be said, Lord Mayor Alderman Charles Walker's statement was short: 'This is an historic occasion. A day for rejoicing. And so it should be. But let us remember those men who are fighting in the Far East, those who are prisoners in Japanese hands, and those who, since 1939, have given their lives in the cause of freedom.' A prayer was followed by the hymn *O God Our Help In Ages Past* and, finally, a rousing version of the National Anthem.

That evening, at Leeds Parish Church on Kirkgate, now Leeds Minster, Reverend Arthur Stretton Reeve, the Vicar of Leeds, presided over another thanksgiving service. In his sermon, he spoke of the hand of God in the victory, of the 'providential' delivery and the 'providential hand of God in the appalling blunders made by the enemy which had contributed so much to their final downfall'. And he declared that, since future historians would say that the years of war would be the 'greatest years in the whole history of our land', the country should strive to 'build a better world for which so many had died'. In both the afternoon and evening, services of Solemn Benediction were attended by large congregations at St Anne's Roman Catholic Cathedral in Cookridge Street, after which the cathedral's organist, Bernard F. Malone, gave a recital of patriotic music.

The *Yorkshire Post* reported that the good folk of Leeds ended an evening of revelry in an orderly fashion. They had celebrated, certainly. Some 2,000 of them had crowded into Victoria Hall, with hundreds more outside, for a special concert at which they had been entertained by Henry Croudson on the organ, and soloists Ernest Broadbent and Gordon Stokes, before joining in community singing.

In general, though, Leeds's celebrations had taken place 'happily, but in moderation' and, as the evening drew to a close, 'it was a well-behaved crowd that queued up for the last tramcars and decided it was better to talk over the events of the day at the fireside than to walk home from town, but here and there bursts of liveliness arose among the smiling people, civilian and Service, who patrolled the city'.

'Down Bond Street came a uniformed piper playing *I'm the Cock of the North* with two rows of people with linked arms following him. He turned toward City Square where the bright floodlights at the Queens Hotel glistened on the great "V" of flags down the front. From a Bond Street restaurant dance music floated through open windows, and now and again an exuberant couple on the pavement dance a few steps together to the strains. Outside the NAAFI club impromptu dancers began for a few minutes and then broke up.'

At Victoria Park in Keighley, a battalion of the Durham Light Infantry had paraded at another open-air service before marching to the decorated Town Hall Square for yet another commemoration. In Bradford, community singing was the order of the day and a huge crowd gathered outside the Town Hall where the police band provided popular tunes, which the younger folk, singing and dancing along, particularly enjoyed. Bradford Cathedral held half-hourly thanksgiving services throughout the day.

In Halifax, crowds gave 'three cheers for Mr Churchill' at the end of a sombre silence and public prayers held in memory of the war dead. Town landmarks like the Wainhouse Tower and Bull Green House were illuminated, and high above the town the beacon shone from Beacon Hill.

The people of Huddersfield were treated to one better, as the *Huddersfield Examiner* reported, 'Hundreds of coloured electric lights twinkled outside the floodlit town hall and in Greenhead Park fairy lights were suspended from the trees in the main walk and on the grass verges were illuminated set pieces – a windmill and the figures of a Dutch boy and girl – and the war memorial was floodlit.' But there was one more treat in store – an illuminated Corporation trolleybus with 'fairy lights, royal blue and gold tasselated bunting and huge victory Vs' travelled over different routes in turn. 'Happy, carefree, singing crowds milled in the streets until midnight and after.'

In Otley, an estimated 3,000 people attended an open-air service in Manor Square. Their singing was led by the mass choirs of the town and accompanied by the band of the Durham Light Infantry. Later, local civil defence services participated in a torchlight procession to the top of the Chevin, a natural ridge overlooking the town, where a bonfire was lit. The folk of Otley, however, were none the wiser, since a dense mist had formed concealing the glow of the bonfire until after midnight.

There was better luck for the people of Wakefield where a huge bonfire was lit in the Bullring in the centre of the town. For most, dancing was the order of the night, and the main roads were closed to traffic. In Dewsbury, where flags were hung around the Market Place, a large crowd gathered in front of the Town Hall to hear the official announcements before the Batley Old Band treated revellers to its musical programme.

Across the wider Leeds area, many special events had been organised for the following day, including a multi-faith service held at Victoria Hall. Some, of course, preferred to be outdoors, and several cricket matches were arranged. One, at Roundhay Park, saw Jack Appleyard's Charity Cricketers take on Eddie Paynter's XI. Another, at Old Park Road in Roundhay, was between North Leeds and Leeds Zingari. A remarkable number of open-air brass band concerts also took place, by the band of the West Yorkshire Regiment at Roundhay Park, at Woodhouse Moor by the Brighouse and Rastrick Band, at North Street Recreation Ground by St Hilda's Band, at Cross Flatts Park by Leeds Model Prize Band, at Gott's Park by the Lockwood Brass Band, and at Stanningley Park by the Armley and Wortley Prize Band. Several of the performances were repeated that evening, with the addition of the Rothwell Temperance Band, who performed at Meanwood Recreation Ground. In addition, the big tops at Roundhay and Woodhouse were opened for free public dancing in the afternoon and evening.

Even local companies were keen to join in the festivities. As well as a Ministry of Food recipe for a chocolate cake made with the dreaded powdered eggs, the pages of the *Yorkshire Post* featured an advertisement from Rowntree's featuring a giant 'V' for victory and illustrations of the flags of the Allies and armed services: 'To the people of Britain and the Empire and to our Allies and all parts of the World we send Victory Greetings and Thanks. We salute the invincible courage and imperishable spirit that has made this year of 1945 the year of Liberation and Peace. Friends and Allies – we salute you.'

In the Nottinghamshire town of Newark, the bells had rung out to celebrate victory, there had been speeches, prayers and rousing cheers, and crowds had gathered in the Market Place to hear the king speak. Like the rest of the town, which the *Newark Advertiser* reported had 'become beflagged overnight', the Town Hall, floodlit for the occasion, was 'dressed with six large flags' – the Union Flag, the Stars and Stripes and the Red Flag – from the flagpoles, and the national flags of China, France and Poland hung from the balcony. Many streets had been festooned with smaller flags and bunting and 'victory archways' had been fashioned from streamers. The highest flag of all, though, flew from the roof of the sugar beet factory chimney to the north of the town. Those intending to take an impromptu dip as part of their celebration were disappointed since the static water tanks that stood in the town's Market Place had been emptied earlier in the week to avoid such an event. Newark Castle was also floodlit that night and had played host to countless children, sporting red, white and blue ribbons and favours, and waving flags and singing as they went along. Shopkeepers had joined in with patriotic window displays including one by a shoe shop owner who had even managed a display of red, white and blue shoes. Pubs, which remained open until 11.30pm, were busy all night long and the mood was described as 'convivial'.

In Derby, 2,000 people went to the town's Market Place to watch a British Legion parade before a violent midday thunderstorm sent them scurrying for cover until the worst of the storm had abated. Alfred Rawlinson, the Bishop of Derby, reminded them, 'We have won a victory over Germany. Be satisfied with that. Don't grumble about the weather.'

By 2pm, the sun was shining again, and the victory celebrations went into full swing. Trolley bus standards were swathed in bunting, and loudspeakers replayed speeches by the king and Winston Churchill. Amateur musicians armed with saxophones and accordions were joined by others with dustbin lids, tin cans and anything else that would make a noise. Everywhere carefully stored-up rations were at last unwrapped as the street parties began.

Yet, in the midst of all this euphoria, there was some bitterness towards the Government after the people had first heard news of Germany's unconditional surrender from German sources only. A bus conductress, on hearing that the Germans had announced their surrender, proclaimed: 'That's good enough for me. I've got a day off!' But a man nearby grumbled: 'We've got it from every country in the world – except our own.' Some railway workers decided not to wait and downed tools. Company officials held a hasty meeting and decided to let the workers go, except for those doing essential work.

Uncertain whether the holiday announcement applied to them, many workers had turned up, only to be sent back home. Outside the Rolls-Royce factory in Derby, where the Merlin aero-engines of Battle of Britain fame had been produced – workers strolled in groups, discussing how to spend the rest of the day.

With so many determined to celebrate, there was some difficulty in making telephone calls – only those placed in an emergency were being connected. Postal services, too, were limited and locals were reassured that things would return to normal the following day. That lack of communication meant that one woman would experience the most unexpected but joyful moment of her life.

Ivy Ryalls of Derby, who since she was eighteen had been doing her bit building torpedoes at the International Combustion company in the town, remembered,

'My husband had been on leave and there'd been a tearful parting because he was going back to the Pacific. He was on the *Illustrious* – the aircraft carrier. On VE Day, it was announced that the war was over, and everyone was in high spirits at work and all the girls said, "Let's go out and celebrate." And we went to the Tiger Bar in the Cornmarket. But I was ever so miserable because I knew he'd set sail and I couldn't see him. So I went home, and I went to bed, and during the night he crawled in at the side of me because the sailing had been cancelled. As far as I was concerned our war had finished and our life had begun.'

Chapter 21

Deliverance for the Channel Islands

The cheering is still going on. It will go on for days. Everybody is happy, apart from the sulky, surly Germans who stand waiting to help unload the food we have brought. The people have left off booing them, now we've arrived.

Harry Proctor, Sunday Dispatch

When the Allies invaded France in June 1944, they left the Channel Islands, just 14 miles (22km) off the Normandy coast, to their fate for another eleven months. German forces there were now isolated and so it was considered that there was no urgency in liberating the 66,000 residents who had chosen to remain after the occupation in 1940, even though they had then faced five years of shortages, especially of food, and oppressive regulations under the Nazis.

So, after D-Day, the islanders would have to wait for almost a year for the arrival of what they would later learn was Task Force 135, a combined force of some 6,000 army and naval personnel who were taking part in Operation Nest Egg, first planned, initially under a different name, in 1943.

Finally, on VE Day, Winston Churchill, in formally announcing to the House of Commons the end of the war against Germany, drew special cheers from MPs, and from peers, diplomats and distinguished strangers in the side galleries, when he told them that 'our dear Channel Islands will be free tomorrow'. The following day, the B-class destroyer HMS *Beagle* brought British troops to Jersey, while her sister ship, HMS *Bulldog*, landed more in Guernsey, and, on 10 May, a declaration of unconditional surrender was signed.

Press Association military correspondent R.A. Eccleston, who was aboard HMS *Bulldog*, was one of several journalists who painted the scene:

'The moment of liberation was preceded by an astonishing story of German obstinacy, of complete lack of dignity in defeat, and finally of a midnight surrender, and a dawn signing of the documents.

'The German surrender ship was a dirty, battered minesweeper. A 3ft x 6ft rubber dinghy was heaved over the side.

'Three Nazi sailors climbed into it, followed by a young naval officer carrying an attaché case. He was not more than twenty-three or twenty-four was the German emissary. Waves soaked him from waist downwards as he came to the *Bulldog* to be received by the click of saluting rifles, and the shrill call of boatswains' whistles. His hand shot out in the Nazi salute. From his attaché case he produced credentials.

'In the wardroom was an impressive array of British officers. There he again presented his credentials, which stated that he had power to receive the armistice terms for conveyance to the German commander-in-chief of the islands. The brigadier turned to the interpreter: "Make it quite clear to him that this is immediate surrender and not an armistice." The German rapped back his reply. He had not the power to sign unconditional surrender but had only come to receive the terms of armistice, and that armistice did not come into force until 00.01 hours next morning.

'He was told to withdraw and later was again summoned to the wardroom to be informed that he would be sent back to his chief with a copy of the instrument of surrender in English and in German, and with instructions that another rendezvous must be arranged forthwith. The German, with astonishing arrogance and stubbornness, said, "I will do that."'

Later that day, the Swedish-owned SS *Vega*, which had been chartered by the Red Cross, arrived in the newly-liberated Channel Islands. It was her fifth voyage since Christmas 1944. She had delivered to the islands a total of 4,344 tonnes of Red Cross supplies. They included 435,032 food parcels, 22,000 special invalid diet parcels, 500 cases of medical supplies, 23 tonnes of soap and 500,000 cigarettes. The total cost to the Red Cross, with shipping and chartering expenses, was estimated to be more than £250,000.

There were many stories to be told to the liberators. The German garrison had received no supplies for many weeks, and locals described how they had seen German soldiers eating earthworms and grass, and how nine of them had battered an old woman when she sought to protect her food. One man in the crowd at St Peter Port said that the cigarette he was smoking had cost him 28 shillings (£1.40). Frank King, a Press Association war correspondent, offered him one of his own cigarettes, and in a frenzied grabbing of hands the entire packet disappeared. It disappeared, said the man, just as all the dogs and cats have disappeared from the island – only those had been eaten.

As the German garrison of Guernsey surrendered, Union Flags and bunting fluttered from every house. Islanders kissed and hugged twenty-two men of the Royal Artillery as they came ashore at St Peter Port, while the *Daily Mirror* reported, 'The one touch of Nazi insolence during the day was when a German motor barge, ordered to take our troops ashore, came alongside the British ships with the Nazi swastika still flying. It didn't fly for long.'

Frank King told of the scene in St Peter Port, where the tiny force of artillerymen formed up on the docks, fixed bayonets and marched towards the dock gates. Behind the gates was a seething cheering, crying crowd of men, women and children. Wrote King,

'Over them the church bells of St Peter Port were clanging tumultuously. Every house had its Union Jack and bunting, saved through five long desperate wearing years for this moment. Then the crowd broke through the gates. In one second those gunners were marching like guardsmen, in the next they were torn from the ranks, kissed hugged cheered … somehow the soldiers reformed, and two girls with great Union Jacks led them into town. People rushed from their houses to join the crowd.

'The joy of people who have been eating rabbit skins, getting one and a half pounds of potatoes each week, who had that morning breakfasted on stewed cabbage leaves, was almost heartbreaking.'

The scenes in Jersey were much the same. *Sunday Dispatch* reporter Harry Proctor told how

'a few hours ago, with 7,000 troops and 90 tons of food, clothes, fuel and equipment, I sailed into St Aubin's Bay and landed in St Helier – this town of holiday memories – sharing with our boys the thrill of being welcomed in a tongue which every Cockney, Midlander, Yorkshireman, and Scotsman could understand'.

'This time we were not wondering what the liberated people were saying, what they were singing. As they showered us with rose petals, flung their arms around our necks, kissed, hugged, and danced before us, we felt that this was the best liberation of the war, for the people we had liberated were our own kith and kin and spoke as we do.'

Allan Nicholson, for the combined press and radio, wired from St Helier:

'British troops in full battle kits scrambled ashore at two principle Jersey ports on Saturday and marched down streets lined with flag-waving and cheering citizens.

'The troops landed in assault landing craft. Offshore lay a miniature armada which brought not only soldiers but civil officials … food and stores for the hungry islanders. The Germans, who by night had withdrawn to prepared areas on the islands, including Alderney, numbered 26,609, and within a few days a start will be made shipping them to prison camps in Britain.'

During the occupation more than 1,000 civilian islanders had been deported to Germany and France to work. Among those freed from German captivity on the islands themselves were workers from other occupied countries that had been brought in against their will to build fortifications as part of the German Atlantic Wall defence. Those from Western Europe and Africa were 'conscripted' and had some freedom, subject to the German curfew. Those with Slavic heritage were regarded simply as slave labour. Many – there were an estimated 1,000 from Russia alone, and also 1,000 French Jews – had suffered brutal treatment, which they had not survived. Reports from Alderney, the most fortified of the Channel Islands, suggested that between 1,000 and 1,200 Russians and Jews had been put to death and buried there. The total has always been hotly contested, but what is a fact is that Channel Islanders had often risked their own lives to help and to hide the workers.

There were many examples of courageous acts. Harry Proctor told the story of one of the 'thousands of heroines in this town'. Pretty 21-year-old Joyce Le Tempier, who had for months been watched by the Germans, had supplied the handful of Allied prisoners of war held in St Hellier with all the news, typing it out and daily visiting their camp to pass it through the barbed wire. 'I had to do something somehow,' said Joyce. 'The Germans got suspicious of me hanging around the camps. But I fooled them every day and got the news through every day.' Proctor wrote, 'Joyce was proud of her pretty legs, clad in silk. "I haven't worn stockings for years," she told me. "They cost me £2 2s 9d [£2.13] and I saved them to wear today."'

Proctor also told of the other side of the coin: 'Remember what happened to the French girls who collaborated with Germans? The islanders here are dealing in their own way with British girls who collaborated. Some have been stripped, tarred and feathered, heads shaved, thrown into duckponds. The British authorities are taking all steps to stop this, but it is still going on in the country part of Jersey.'

Pearl Vardon was a 25-year-old schoolteacher living in St Helier when the Germans invaded. She spoke German and in 1941 was forced to work for the Organisation Todt, an engineering confederation that provided labour for the fortification of the Channel islands. She fell in love with a German officer, Siegfried Carl Schwatlo, and, when he was posted back to Germany, she followed him and took work as a broadcaster of propaganda with German-controlled Radio Luxemburg and in Germany with Reichs-Rundfunk. In

1945, she was arrested by British forces at Wilhelmshaven. 'She is a British subject and probably a traitor,' concluded a British intelligence officer. In February 1946, at the Old Bailey, Vardon pleaded guilty to six charges concerning broadcasting for the enemy. She was sentenced to a relatively lenient nine months' imprisonment, although the MI5 report on Vardon said that 'her motive seems to have been the clear one of avoiding as much as possible separation from the German officer with whom she fell in love … It is just possible that her motives were not so simple as they appear to have been on the surface'. Whatever, in 1950, in Abergavenny, she married her lover. Vardon died in Bavaria in November 2011, aged 96.

As Vardon was being interrogated in Germany, *Sunday Dispatch* journalist F.B. McGarry perhaps best summed up the atmosphere on that day of liberation in her native Channel Islands: 'The loudest cheer at St Peter Port, when the main British force arrived, was not for the thousands of soldiers armed to the teeth, who got their share, but for one austere Londoner. He walked up from the first assault craft, firmly holding his bowler on his head with his left hand, clutching his tightly-rolled umbrella with the right hand, and at the same time obviously concerned about the dispatch case under his right arm. The dispatch case carried by a civil servant, Mr C.D. Bickmore, was important because in it were some of the plans for the complete rehabilitation of this half-starved community.

'It was the bowler hat and the umbrella that brought tears to these island eyes and the cry of "There'll always be an England", followed by a roar of cheers mixed with the laughter of semi hysterical happiness.'

When, on 7 June 1945, one year and one day after D-Day, King George VI – the 'Duke of Normandy' – and Queen Elizabeth arrived off Jersey in the cruiser HMS *Jamaica* from Portsmouth, some 300 German prisoners asked to be allowed to line part of the route to welcome them. They were refused, and half an hour before the royal party arrived were herded into lorries and driven from the quayside. The king and queen were greeted by the Bailiff, Alexander Coutanche, and Brigadier Alfred Snow, the commander of Task Force 135. After a tour of the island, the royal couple arrived at the Royal Court and States Chamber in St Helier, where they heard a red-robed official announce in Norman French, 'Les etats sont complets,' and the islanders knew that, after years of Nazi rule, their own parliament was once more.

The royal couple then made the short flight to Guernsey aboard a Dakota of Transport Command with a fighter escort of Spitfires.

Victor Lewis, the Manchester *Daily Dispatch* special correspondent, told readers: 'German prisoners helped to welcome the King and Queen when they made their postponed air, sea and land tour of the liberated Channel

Islands today. As the royal plane touched down on the airport in Guernsey this afternoon, a salute was fired from captured German field guns.

'Several days ago, some of the German prisoners, still kept on the island to clear mines, were put to making ammunition. They were told it was to be used for the royal salute and were asked whether they were prepared to do it. Every German said he would like to, and today, from a far corner of the island, where they had been put ... they heard their guns giving honour to our King and Queen ... Nearly 60,000 islanders have today seen their King and Queen for the first time, and on every corner and outside every house on the route, the King, wearing the uniform of an admiral of the fleet, and the Queen, in beige, were cheered. The children threw flowers into their open car and at one point that possession drove over a fifty-yard carpet of wild flowers laid in the roadway by schoolchildren.'

The queen paused to chat with seven members of the Queens' Institute of District Nurses, who had insisted on remaining to look after the sick after the German occupation, and the king and queen left their car to inspect a parade of the British Legion and to talk to French ex-servicemen who had fought in the First World War.

In an open-air ceremony in the Candie Gardens, the loyal address was read by the Bailiff, Sir Victor Carey, and the Dame of Sark, Sybil Hathaway, also gave an address. The *Newcastle Journal* said, 'The King and Queen looked over the heads of a great concourse of people to the blue sea sparkling in the sun with Sark lying in the distance.' Then the royal couple, still escorted by Spitfires, flew home, to RAF Northolt and from there were driven to Buckingham Palace, leaving Channel Islanders to look back on a day that had set the seal on their liberation.

Epilogue

The war in the Far East is over and may peace soon return to this distracted world ... The end has come not a day too soon.
Dr Bernard Griffin, Roman Catholic Archbishop of Westminster

On 26 July 1945, the people of Britain learned that they had a new government. Eight weeks earlier, following the Allies' victory in Europe, the coalition that Winston Churchill set up in 1940 had been dissolved. The Labour Party, now anxious to fight a general election for the first time in a decade, had withdrawn its support. Since the 1935 general election, there had been a huge change in the public's outlook. The *Beveridge Report*, published in 1942, recommended a comprehensive welfare system that included a national health service. William Beveridge's plans enjoyed widespread support, but not from Churchill and the Conservative Party, whose reaction was, at best, lukewarm. With Germany defeated, the Labour leader, Clement Attlee, wanted to put the new left-leaning agenda to the ultimate test. Churchill had wanted to wait until the war in the Pacific was won before calling the election, but, when Attlee walked away, he had no choice but to go to the country.

Election day in Britain was 5 July, but the results were not announced until three weeks later, to allow servicemen and women stationed overseas to vote. Churchill had banked on his popularity as the nation's wartime leader – 'Vote National – Help Him Finish The Job' was the slogan – but, in a speech on 4 June, he attacked the Labour Party in a way that astonished even his own supporters: 'No socialist government conducting the entire life and industry of the country could afford to allow free, sharp, or violently-worded expressions of public discontent. They would have to fall back on some form of Gestapo, no doubt very humanely directed in the first instance.'

The word 'Gestapo' leapt out, and Attlee seized upon it: 'Make no mistake, it has only been through the power of the State, given to it by Parliament, that the general public has been protected against the greed of ruthless profit-makers and property owners. The Conservative Party remains, as always, a class party. In twenty-three years in the House of Commons, I cannot recall more than half a dozen from the ranks of the wage earners. It represents today, as in the past, the forces of property and privilege.' Attlee reminded voters that Churchill, their wartime leader, was now simply Churchill, the leader of the Conservative Party, and 'I thank him for having disillusioned them so thoroughly'.

Despite opinion polls showing Labour six points ahead of the Tories, there was only guarded optimism in Labour ranks. When the early results came in, however, they gave cause for hope that the pollsters had been correct. Leo Amery and Brendan Bracken, two of Churchill's most loyal supporters, had lost their seats.

There were many more shocks to come and, when everything had been added up, Labour had a Commons majority of 146 seats with 47.8 per cent of the vote and an 11.8 swing in their favour. Hugh Gaitskell, Harold Wilson, James Callaghan, Michael Foot, Barbara Castle and Denis Healey were among the Labour faces entering Parliament for the first time. The number of Conservative MPs had dropped from 387 to 197. The Liberals were reduced to twelve MPs. Churchill was reported to be astounded, but the man who had led Britain through a world war was not seen as the man to lead Britain in peacetime.

In 1935, there had been 31.3 million eligible voters, 21.9 million of whom cast their vote. In 1945, some 25 million out of 33.2 million voted. In those ten years, Labour's aggregate popular vote had grown by 10 per cent. Tens of thousands of first-time voters had had their say. There were several successful fringe candidates, and, taking political leanings more generally, the *Birmingham Daily Post* reckoned that, if one counted in Liberals, Independent Labour Party, Commonwealth, Communist and Independents against the Tories, National Liberals and Nationals, then the Left had a majority of 210. Whichever way one chose to interpret it, voters in the 1945 General Election had delivered a crushing blow to Winston Churchill.

Just as Churchill had warned, two months earlier, that the German surrender did not mean that Britons could forget 'the toils and efforts that lie ahead', so his successor also had some sobering words. Peace heralded not days of plenty, but even greater austerity. In August 1945, the US government's abrupt and unexpected ending of Lend-Lease, the programme whereby the Americans provided food, raw materials including oil, medical supplies and clothing, not to mention warships, warplanes and weapons, to its Allies, meant major cuts in imports, while goods meant for home consumption would now have to be exported.

The Potsdam Conference of July–August 1945 continued the discussions held between the 'Big Three' – Winston Churchill (replaced by Clement Attlee after the general election), Harry Truman (the new US president after the death of Franklin D. Roosevelt) and Joseph Stalin – at Yalta the previous February, to determine the post-war borders of Europe. There were inevitable disagreements, but one matter that was settled was the future of Germany, which would now be split into four zones of Allied Occupation: British, American, Russian and French.

Russian newspaper readers got their first view of the new British prime minister, photographed standing next to Truman, in *Krasnaya Zvezda* ('Red Star'), the official newspaper of the Soviet Ministry of Defence, noting that the British Labour Party advocated closer co-operation among the Big Three: 'It would be dangerous if there were no general line and if in all four areas of occupation there were no co-ordinated policy.'

On 15 August 1945, Britain celebrated VJ Day. Officially the war still had a few days to run because the Japanese would not surrender with a signed document until 2 September, but the dropping of two atomic bombs on their country, on 6 and 9 August, had signalled the end. The Soviet Union had declared war on Japan on 8 August. 'Probably the last straw from the Russian point of view,' commented the *Birmingham Mail*, 'has been the atomic bomb, which has put behind the Potsdam call to surrender by a force unsuspected even by Russia until Hiroshima and now Nagasaki felt the impact of Allied power. This greatest of all wars is ending with a supreme demonstration of the price of perfidy and aggression.'

As with VE Day, there were street parties – in Offerton Avenue in Derby, children burned an effigy of the Japanese warlord Togo – and in London's Chinatown American GIs joined civilians in singing and dancing and lighting a bonfire. Crowds in front of Buckingham Palace stretched from the Queen Victoria Memorial back along the Mall to beyond Admiralty Arch. The king and queen and the two princesses attended a thanksgiving service at St Paul's Cathedral, while people crowded into Whitehall and into Downing Street, where Clement Attlee received a cheer.

In many towns and cities, though, celebrations at the end of the war in the Far East were muted – at midnight on VJ Day, a huge crowd in Derby's Market Place sang *Abide With Me* before falling into a two-minutes silence to remember the dead – because many families still did not know the fate of loved ones who, in the months after D-Day, had still been fighting – or had been imprisoned – there. Altogether, more than 170,000 men serving in the UK armed forces had been captured by German or Italian forces. Some were airmen whose aircraft had been shot down while on bombing raids on German cities. Some were sailors whose vessels had been sunk and who had been pulled from the sea. Most of them, however, were soldiers who had been captured after defeats in France, North Africa and the Balkans between 1940 and 1942. In comparison to the fate of the 6 million Russian soldiers taken prisoner by the Germans, British, Commonwealth and American POWs were treated relatively well. They suffered boredom, hunger and deprivation, and occasional acts of cruelty, but the Russians, together with Jewish prisoners and those suspected of being Communists, were routinely starved and brutalised. Some 3.3 million Russians died in German POW camps. Unlike Western prisoners of war, they were considered by their captors as subhuman.

On VE Day, more than 13,000 British prisoners of war had been brought home in 200 Lancaster bombers and, by the end of May, an estimated 156,000 had been repatriated from camps in Italy and Germany. At teatime on VE Day, the Harrison family of Middleton Street in Derby received a great surprise. Through the door, to the delight of his wife and family, came Corporal Sid Harrison of the RASC. Forty-four-year-old Corporal Harrison had made his way home from a German POW camp, where he had been since his capture in 1941. Over the next few days, similar scenes were played out throughout the country.

On 14 May, two brothers, Sergeant Alister Anderson of the Royal Signals, and Lance-corporal Richard Anderson of the RASC, who had both been prisoners of war in German camps, arrived together at their home in Esslemont Avenue in Aberdeen. Lance-corporal Anderson had been taken prisoner at El Michili in Libya in April 1941. His brother was captured at Tobruk in September the following year. Later, they met in a camp at Pavma in Italy. When the Italian armistice came in 1943, both escaped. They made their way towards the Allies and were within 14 miles (22km) of the British lines when they were recaptured by the Germans. They were transferred to Stalag VIIA in Germany, where they remained until they were released by American forces.

In September, following the Japanese surrender, it was the turn of 200,000 military prisoners and civilian internees to be returned home from the Far East. About 30,000 had died in Japanese camps, at 20 per cent a death rate seven times that of German camps. It would be some time before families knew if their hopes and prayers had been answered.

There were happy homecomings, of course, but for many the world would never be the same. Years of fighting in the jungle or being held in captivity, often in the most barbaric conditions, had changed them; and in different ways, the war had also changed the ones they had left behind. There would be so many problems for servicemen as they re-entered civilian life after experiencing such horrors, but Newcastle *Sunday Sun* columnist Lewis Ashley picked up on one that perhaps few had considered:

'We all know of colonels and squadron leaders who, before the war, were not entrusted with anything more important than looking after the office stamps or doing the hack work that their seniors dodged. How are all these fine men who have proved themselves to be first-class leaders in the stern test of war going to be re-established into Civvy St? Are they to begin again where they left off, or is it possible to find jobs for them carrying something like the responsibilities they showed in uniform? This week a Southport policeman will be returning to work. Only twenty-nine and a ranker when he enlisted, he left the Army as a lieutenant-colonel. Now he is going back cheerfully to his £5-a-week job as a constable …'

The Second World War claimed the lives of more than 384,000 British soldiers, sailors and airmen, who died in combat, and those of nearly 70,000 civilians; 40,000 civilians died in the seven-month period of the Blitz between September 1940 and May 1941, almost half of them in London. The United States lost 407,000 servicemen. The conflict cost Germany 4.3 million of its forces (3.2 million known dead; 1.2 million missing) and 2.1 million civilians, although the figures have been challenged and depend on a number of factors. Again, depending on which study one chooses, the Soviet Union lost between 8.7 million and 14 million of its military. Worldwide, between 50 million and 80 million people were killed as a result of the war. The exact figure can never be established.

Among all the horrors, though, there were many happy stories, and the last year of the Second World War ended on a lighter note for those of a romantic disposition. On 31 December 1945, the *Sunderland Daily Echo and Shipping Gazette* reported, 'So many British soldiers are marrying Italian girls that a special department has been set up to deal with the problem, says Reuters from Rome. The problem of transporting these Italian brides to their new homes in Britain is being sorted out. The British soldier who wishes to marry an Italian girl has to wait a stipulated time before he can lead her to the altar. Apart from the ecclesiastical tangles arising from the marriage of a Protestant to a Catholic – as is the case in the majority of these marriages – the soldier must undergo a waiting period stipulated by the Army.

'This waiting period was originally at the discretion of the commanding officer, but last September was fixed at a maximum of two months. Previously the soldier and his Italian girl were separated during the waiting period, but the futility of such an arrangement eventually prevailed upon the Army authorities and the couple can now be together.'

As 1946 dawned, Germany was a nation defeated and divided, its people struggling through the bitterest of winters in towns and cities bombed to ruins. In England, the first snow fell in mid-December, and it would be the end of March before the weather released its grip, which meant hard work for many Axis prisoners of war who were used to clear roads and dig through to isolated villages. Their efforts were not always appreciated. German POWs helping to shift snow from a railway line in Wales were pelted with stones by angry locals.

Animosity was not always the case, however, and it was sport that helped to heal the wounds. In 1946, the Devon village of Bradworthy raised a team to play German POWs from the local camp. The Germans, who included former professionals in their ranks, won 10–1. At Poppylot POW camp in Feltwell, Norfolk, the prisoners were mostly infantrymen aged from twenty-five upwards. They had a very good football team and played against other camps. On one occasion, they, too, met the village team, on the prisoners' 'home' ground, a farmer's field opposite the camp. Footballing prisoners of war were not confined just to village life, though. Brian Harris was an 11-year-old London schoolboy in 1946: 'I remember regularly playing football with the German POWs who were housed in Richmond Park. The gates were left open so they could come and go as they pleased. It was better than going back home to Germany, I suppose.'

A week before VE Day, a *Western Morning News* leader writer had commented on reports that the Germans, on the brink of defeat, were better fed than the British, and that, unless something was done to address the issue, herein lay a problem for the future:

> 'If anybody is in danger of forgetting that when Germany is down she must be resolutely kept down, it is worthwhile to call attention to an aspect of the situation which will matter very much in twenty years' time. Our soldiers overrunning Germany have found the population well fed. This is very striking contrast to the famished populations of the greater part of Europe. The nutritional condition of the Germans at present is far better than our own and vastly better than that of Continental countries. This means that if there were any relaxation of our vigilance, then the Germans, as a result of their own misdeeds, would start the next war with very definite biological advantage over their victims. This is a state of affairs which we could not possibly have avoided. We believe there are few people who do not resent our pedantic adherence to the Geneva Conventions after the enemy had flouted them. It is an outrage that German prisoners should be better fed than our own civil population. Nobody, however, will suggest that we could or should have instituted

a policy of deliberately starving prisoners. There are certain directions in which those who are completely inhumane have advantages of which they cannot be deprived. It should go without saying that in the limited supplies of food available after the war, Germany's claims will come after those of everybody else.'

In July 1946, bread would be rationed for the first time in Britain …

Bibliography

Books

Beevor, Antony, *Berlin: The Downfall, 1945* (London, Viking, 2002)

Dollinger, Hans, *The Decline and Fall of Nazi Germany and Imperial Japan* (London, Bounty Books, 1997)

Eisenhower, Dwight D., *Crusade in Europe* (New York, Doubleday, 1948)

Gregg, Victor, *Rifleman: A Front-Line Life from Alamein and Dresden to the Fall of the Berlin Wall* (London, Bloomsbury, 2011)

Haining, Peter, *The Flying Bomb War* (London, Robson Books, 2002)

Linge, Heinz, *With Hitler To The End: The Memoirs of Adolf Hitler's Valet* (Barnsley, Frontline Books, 2013)

Makepeace, Clare, *Captives of War: British Prisoners of War in Europe in the Second World War* (Cambridge, Cambridge University Press, 2017)

Misch, Rochus, *Hitler's Last Witness: The Memoirs of Hitler's Bodyguard* (Barnsley, Frontline Books, 2014)

Rippon, Anton, *Gas Masks For Goal Posts: Football in Britain During The Second World War* (Stroud, Sutton Publishing, 2005).

Rippon, Anton, *How Britain Kept Calm and Carried On* (London, Michael O'Mara Books, 2014).

Scovell, Brian, *Learie, The Man Who Broke the Colour Bar* (Leicestershire, The Book Guild, 2021)

Snyder, Louis L., *Hitler and Nazism* (London, Bantam Books, 1967)

Speer, Albert, *Inside The Third Reich* (London, The Macmillan Company, 1970)

Ward, Andrew, *Armed With a Football* (Oxford, Crowberry, 1994)

Wheal, Elizabeth Anne, and Pope, Stephen, *The Macmillan Dictionary of the Second World War, second edition* (London, Macmillan, 1997)

Newspapers and Magazines

Aberdeen Evening Express, Aberdeen Press and Journal, Ballymena Daily Telegraph, Belfast Telegraph, Birmingham Mail, Birmingham Post, Burton Daily Mail, Burton Observer, Dagens Nyhete, Daily Dispatch, Daily Express, Daily Herald, Daily Mirror, Daily News, Daily Record, Daily Telegraph, Das Reich, Derby Evening Telegraph, Deutsche Allgemeine Zeitung, Dumfries and Galloway Standard, Dundee Courier, Eastbourne Chronicle, Essex Chronicle, Gloucestershire Echo, Halifax Evening Courier, Hampshire Telegraph, Hartlepool Northern Daily Mail, Huddersfield Examiner, Hull Daily Mail, Illustrated London News, Journal de Genève, Kent and Sussex Courier, Krasnaya Zvezda, Lancashire Daily Post, Leicester Evening Mail, Lincolnshire Echo, Liverpool Daily Post, Londonderry Sentinel, Los Angeles Times, Manchester Evening News, New York Times, Newcastle Evening Chronicle, News Chronicle, Newcastle Journal, Nottingham Evening Post, Nottingham Journal, Pontypridd Observer, Rochdale Observer, Sternenbanner, Sunday Dispatch, Sunday Express, Sunday Pictorial, Sunday Post, Sunday Sun, Sunderland Daily Echo and Shipping Gazette, Skegness News, The People, The Scotsman, Völkischer Beobachter, West Sussex Gazette, Western Mail, Western Morning News, Wisden Cricketers' Almanack, Yorkshire Observer, Yorkshire Post.

Index